The Truth We Already Knew

A Letter to my Precious Tera Linda

From

Jim W. Evans (Dad)

Library of Congress Cataloging-in-Publication Data

Evans, Jim W.
The Truth We Already Knew: A Letter to My Precious Tera Linda/ Jim W. Evans p. cm.
Include Bibliographical references and appendix.
ISBN 978-0-578-72507-9
1. Christian Life. 2.Family-Christian. 3. Personal Growth-Christian. 2020

LCCN: 2020913801

Dedication

I dedicate this letter to those who inspired me to write: my master teachers, Him, my Mother Joyce, my Grandpa Eddie, Grandma Mae, Preacher/Evangelist Dr. Billy C. Lawrence, and my children, Tera, Jimmie, Michael, and Randall. Without their love and affection, I would never have attempted this work. Also, I thank my nephew Justin D. Morgan for his translation services. He and his family are currently fulfilling a 10-year mission commitment in Arequipa, Peru. Thank you all.

I initially began writing this letter for my daughter and first-born child; however, as I progressed, I started thinking of things I needed to share not only with Tera but also with Jimmie, Michael, and Randall. Finally, it occurred to me that perhaps others could benefit by sharing what was once considered very personal. These writings are from an average guy in this world, not unlike yourself. I have no mastery over the topics of which I speak, but I hope my observations will inspire you as the reader to awaken your curiosity and ask and search out profound truths.

I wish my children, my grandchildren, my extended family, and my guest readers success in discovering truth and meaning in this life.

Table of Contents

(Biblical references are from New Language Translation unless otherwise noted.)

Prologue

Para mi preciosa Tierra Linda,

To my precious Tera Linda,

OH DARLING, WHERE HAS THE TIME GONE? IT SEEMS like only yesterday; I held you so proudly in my oh so trembling arms for the first time. I know that sounds terribly cliché, but I always speak my mind. When I asked you why you were leaving so soon, you said that we had been discussing it for months; I suppose we have, but it seemed to be only in theory. I had no idea this day would come so soon. Tera, I think I must be in shock; has it been 18 years already?!

During the past several days, since you left, I've had so many odd thoughts and remembrances silly little things, like when we used to go shopping for groceries, and Mint Milano cookies would appear in the cart. Or when getting into the car, I was always reaching for the seat positioning controls because thanks to our constant battle of where the seat belongs, but now it is just still where I left it. There have been several times I was about to make a phone call; I was *sure* I heard you in your room on the phone. I would instinctively march toward your bedroom only to remember that you were no longer here. And if you want to hear something really strange, sometimes I opened the door anyway, just to confirm that you were not tying up the phone line like you always did. Am I becoming a tired old man, or am I just missing the sweetest daughter ever? My sweet daughter? I will let you decide, but I suspect the latter.

The most powerful emotion I have ever experienced in my life was when I first held you in my arms. I distinctly remember that very moment when your Mother handed you to me. You still had blood and other fluids covering your body, and you smelled of the strange odor, which may have been a little sickening, but to me, it was wonderful. I remember that moment, captured in time, to this day; I doubt I will ever forget that fragrance. My love for you is larger than my body and caused my chest to ache with joy. The first few months of your life were all-consuming. After a week, I returned to work, but as soon as the day was over, I returned to my happy little family. It was the best time of my life. Now don't get me wrong; the births of your brothers were extraordinary events, but I suppose you, being my first-born child, was an even *more* significant event, one that a father can only try to express.

I think it not fair that most people do not recall memories of their early childhood; your mom and I, and you and your brothers, had so much fun in the beginning. I withdrew from college and went to work in construction so that I could support my young family and spend as much time with you as possible. Every weekend was an adventure; we would go to parks and zoos, rivers and lakes, and even to the ocean! Without exception, I would say that from the time you were born until your mom left our family when you were around nine and a half years old – rain or snow, fog or sunshine – we were off on an adventure every weekend. These incredible adventures continued even when I decided to move from Oregon to Tennessee to attend college, and then again after we moved to Texas for graduate school. Of course, you remember that things changed while we were in Texas after your Mother took off and left. That is when I withdrew from graduate school and started to bounce from job to job. But, we still went to parks often as we could, but it just wasn't the same; at least it was not for me. I am genuinely sorry for that, Tera. I wish I were one of those resilient people who, no matter what happened, kept going and going, like the Energizer bunny. To be very honest with you, and to my embarrassment, I confess that when your mom left, it felt like half of me died. Honestly, if it were not for you kids, I think I would have just hung up my boots and died. I hope that doesn't hurt you, Tera, but you are older now, and I think you can understand both my pain and my neverending love for you and your brothers.

Hindsight is 20/20, and looking back, I see that hard times brought me some benefits. I hope you can appreciate what I am about to share with you. No matter how terrible a situation may seem, *it is only temporary*. Have you heard the saying, "suicide is a permanent solution to a temporary problem?" In life, there are ups, and there are downs, and if you find yourself in a valley, hold on because a mountaintop is around the corner. If you had given up all hope in the valley, you would be embarrassed in front of God when everything finally works out. Hold on to these words, my Love.

I miss you so much, Tera, but I am also so happy for you. I remember when I first left my Mother's home. I was fearless. It never crossed my mind that I would one day fail or get hurt, and to be honest, I did not understand my mom's concern. Oh, how the tides have turned! I am concerned for you, but I am not afraid for you; that is what I tell myself. But why did you have to choose San Francisco? Yes, it is a beautiful city, but Oh the crazies which must live there! Do I sound like a doddering old fool? I hope you will peer through the words and blinds and see the love and caring I have for you. What it is you are seeking, is precisely what I wish for you to find; may your adventure be all that you had hoped.

Now that you are an adult, I would like to share with you a passion of mine, and please listen. I am a man of few passions, or perhaps many, I am not sure? I have not had the occasion with you to speak about what I intend to share with you. All my life, or at the least most of it, from the time I was a young adolescent, I have actively involved myself in the pursuit of the knowledge of mysterious things or things that seemed mysterious to me. Some labeled me in my youth as gifted; however, at the age I now am, and not having contributed in any significant manner to the world in which I find myself, I heavily discount that notion. If one was to call me curious, I believe I would accept that label. As far back as I can remember, I have been prone to daydreaming. Not the aimless mental wonderings, as many of my schoolteachers, assumed; I found myself to present date in deep concentrations on specific thoughts to the negligence of current goings-on, even unto the point of self-endangerment. I have awoken as it were to the prompting of associates, to beware of impending situations.

I hope that you do not misunderstand me. Yet, not all my passionate thinking carries possible peril! It is just that I can, at times, become too preoccupied with my thoughts. Mostly, I would have to say there are a few subjects which I have allowed myself to ponder and I have discovered interesting and useful. I have an affinity for history, science, politics, philosophy, and religion. I say philosophy or religion because my study of philosophy *led me* to the study of religion.

I can almost hear you saying out loud as you read this letter, what does all this have to do with me? Honestly, my sweetheart, I am not sure how it happened, but somewhere along the way, I forgot; overlooked the opportunities I had to share with you some of the things I have learned. There were several small events during your childhood, which indicated to me that you had a bit of your Father's curiosity within you; however, and somehow, I let time getaway, and I never sat you down to discuss these lofty matters. I did share a lot of my thoughts with your Mother; however, considering events as they unfolded, I suspect that she only politely listened and didn't understand or give credence to their gravity.

When you began packing up your belongings and told me that you and your friend had decided to move to the City, a panic set ablaze in me; I began to ask myself if I had taught you everything which I intended to. Have I shared with you all the ideas and discoveries in life which were important to me? Truthfully, the answer came back a resounding no! No, I have not had all the conversations which I meant to have with you. I was not ready for this day to come so soon. So, what am I supposed to do? Do I just let you leave and hope you figure all of life's mysteries on your own? Well, maybe if I were only one of those together parents, who seemed always to know what to do or say, sadly, I am not one of them. I am your Dad. I did the best I could, and I say that with a clear conscious. I readily admit that it may not have been good enough. I wanted you and the boys to have a happy, loving family, and I tried to teach you everything I could so that you would have a head start in this thing that we call life. It did not turn out the way I planned. Some of that was your mom's fault, and some of that was mine. I am sorry for what was lacking, but I hope you know this; my intentions were out of love, honorable, and perfect. What I set out to do for you was to be the perfect Father. I hope you will allow me to attach this addendum to your life teaching and make it more complete. As your Father, I can do no less!

Please be patient with me as I share with you my step-by-step learning adventure; I think you will enjoy my clumsy trek. I began this years ago for myself, and as I grew, I began to pursue it vigorously for my lovely children. Nothing would please me more than if you picked up this legacy and made it yours for your children, my grandchildren. But I am getting ahead of myself.

SECTION 1

WHERE DID THIS ALL COME FROM

Chapter 1

The Cosmos, Earth, and Man

Si valoramos la búsqueda de la sabiduría,
tenemos que estar disponibles de seguir a donde
sea que esa búsqueda nos guíe. La mente libre
no es un perro ladrando que necesita estar
atado con una cadena de 3 metros
— Adlai Stevenson, Discurso, Universidad de
Wisconsin, Madison (8 de Octubre, 1952).

If we value the pursuit of knowledge, we must
be free to follow wherever that search may
lead us. The free mind is no barking dog, to be
tethered on a ten-foot chain.
— Adlai Stevenson, Speech, University of
Wisconsin, Madison (Oct. 8, 1952).

AUTHENTIC LEARNING IS DISCOVERING ABSOLUTE REALITY, whether it is by observation, interaction, intuitive rationalism, or the clever combining of methods; sometimes, if we are humble, it may be by generous revelation. I have stalked this elusive game since youth. Whether or not I have been successful, I leave that for you to judge.

I remember a distinct grinding sound as the wheel spun around a sound like crushing sand. The autumn sun warmed my face, and a gentle breeze lifted my fine curly blonde hair off my brow as I concentrated in earnest on my observations. Alternately, I would bite into my dripping peanut butter and corn syrup sandwich and then feverishly paw at my wagon wheel. I often turned my Radio Flyer wagon upside down to use as a seat, but today as I sat, I was wondrously enthralled with the exploration of how ball bearings allowed the wheel to roll to impossible speeds. Of all the memories from my childhood, this one fills me with the purest sense of contentment, joy, and innocence. I believe I was three or four years old. I do not recall how old I was when I first pondered the origins of the world and everything therein; however, I do remember that when I began to think about these things, I felt changed somehow. However, the stronger feeling was not the change itself; it was the knowledge that I could never go back to the way I was. The simple act of questioning origins shattered the foundations of *my* Nirvana. I do not intend to disturb your peace, but instead, I wish you to join me in the search for reality so that we may enjoy true peace and joy and contentment in our lives.

By the time I started junior high school or what is currently called middle school, I had attended ten different elementary schools. Therefore, it is difficult for me to remember how old I was when I made the jump from curiosity about the world to questioning its origin. I remember that it was before 7th grade. I seem to remember that I was riding a bicycle when I decided that before the world was here, there was nothing. At first, I thought that the universe came from something, but then I realized that "the something" would then have to have come from something else; that thought could go on and on forever, and then the world would have never been! I know that sounds backward, but think as you wish, I was a kid. You may find this unbelievable, after all these years; I have been unable to improve the logic of that first observation. First, there was nothing; then, there was something (formally referred to as space, time and matter, and energy). What else is there to say? The greatest minds from ancient history to modern times have been unable to answer this first question of origin.

If my first question concerns the origin of the "stuff" then, the second question is, how did the "stuff" become all of which we know? Contrary to what you might suspect, I was not an avid reader. I had an aversion to anything academic, having only read two books in this young age: Ben W. Hunt's Indian Crafts and Lore[1], and The Art of Clear Thinking, written by Rudolf Flesch[2]. My aversion toward reading probably had to do with frequent relocating. (How could have I possibly forgotten my very favorite book, The Pokey Little Puppy by Janette Sebring Lowrey![3]) Therefore, it wasn't until years later when my Mother rushed me off to college, I came face to face with academia, and I began to hear the names of scientists, philosophers, and other giants of the academic realm, that I took up the second question of origin.

Carl Sagan simply stated in the first line of his book Cosmos,[4] "The Cosmos is all that there is or ever was or will be." I would say he successfully dodged a bullet. Not so, when it comes to physicist Sir Fredrick Hoyle. In 1949, he was the first to use the phrase "Big Bang Theory." [5] He suggested that at the beginning, there existed a state of pure energy in a vacuum without space or time – then there was a chance fluctuation owing to quantum uncertainty (you know, in the field of all possibilities, etc.). During this moment of singularity, it appears that there were many violations of scientific law.

Considering the First Law of Thermal Dynamics, which states that matter or energy can neither be created nor destroyed, the Big Bang theory purports that a tiny bubble of space-time formed. Within this bubble, the theory states a sort of negative pressure expanded faster than the speed of light. Currently, this is how matter and energy define space and time. Science says that this was the beginning of the cosmos. By mathematical extrapolation of various measurements governed by Newton's three Laws of Motion, they contend that this occurred 15 billion years ago. The Second Law of Thermal Dynamics (disorder increases) accounts for the current observations of the expansion of the universe, which lends support to the origins of our universe, beginning with a great bang. However, it is that pesky Third Law of Thermal Dynamics, which has some people worried. All molecular movement stops at absolute zero: 0 degrees Kelvin, -273.16 degrees Celsius, or -459.68 degrees Fahrenheit (P.S. Even at zero, there is molecular movement. Oh well, it was a good guess.) In theory, the universe and everything in it is expanding at a constant rate following Newton's Laws of Motion. Recently observations of distant supernovae are not adhering to Hubble's law concerning the shift of light-waves toward the red end of the light spectrum (this is called a redshift) as expected. One prominent explanation is that the expansion rate of the universe is increasing due to a mysterious repulsive force. Another notable explication for this puzzling occurrence is that the speed of light is also slowing. I wonder, does this indicate that the rate of the expansion is also decelerating? Would not that be a violation of one of the Laws of Motion? Would it not be a violation of one of the Laws of Thermal Dynamics too? Maybe the "Big Bang" (explosion) is going to end in a "Big Crush" (implosion.) But don't worry; even though the sun is suffering from an ailment known as Heat Death, it has only diminished 2 percent during these previous 15 billion years, according to the experts.

I would be remiss if I failed to tell you that later in his life, Sir Fredrick Hoyle concluded:

".... Once we see, however, that the probability of life originating at random is so utterly minuscule as to make it absurd, it becomes sensible to think that the favorable properties of physics on which life depends are in every respect deliberate. ... It is therefore almost inevitable that our own measure of intelligence must reflect... higher intelligences... even to the limit of God... such a theory is so obvious that one wonders why it is not widely accepted as being self-evident." [6]

The field of Physics and its cousins did not offer me any insight. Accordingly, I turned to the areas of Chemistry and Biology. I thought if I could not find the origins of the universe, perhaps, I could learn how its primordial inhabitants began. I was not disappointed in the sense that there were many theories to study. The most popular was the theory of evolution. However, the study and expansion of Darwinism led to the weakening of his argument; its development weakened the original Darwinism so that it is no longer compatible.[7] I suspect Darwin's influence will wane over the next few years, let us wait and see.

It is my opinion the most exciting scientific feat was accomplished by Dr. Stanley L. Miller (known as the Father of exobiology) in Chicago during the 1950s. Exobiology is the study of the origin of life, the study of life beyond Earth, the study of prebiotic Earth, and what chemical reactions might have taken place as the setting for life's origin. When he placed some gases and water vapor in a vacuum and introduced an electrical charge, he precipitated amino acids known to be the building blocks of life. This result led some to theorize that life on Earth may have originated similarly, however; it still fails to account for the origins of gases, water and electricity.[8]

At this point in my life, I met your Mother and withdrew from college after only completing my first year. My family and your Mother's family were less than enthusiastic about our decisions; nonetheless, for the next five years, we indulged ourselves almost exclusively with the pleasures of young love and a young family. During these years, the appetite of my curious search was most entirely and joyously distracted. By the mid-'80s, our family and financial obligations were growing, and it seemed like a good time to continue my education. It was at this time we moved to West Tennessee, where I first heard of the 'Anthropic Principle'.[9] The scientific community had become awestruck by the delicacy and complexity of the balance of all areas of time, space, matter, and energy making up our natural world. Some developed the principle to demonstrate intelligent design behind all existence. For some, these thoughts purported proof of God; however, I felt this was presumptuous.

I agreed that there was an event of some kind at the beginning of everything, and there is plenty of evidence for intelligent design, but this only suggested some sort of creative force. If this force was to interact with its Creation, would it be appropriate to regard it as God? Has this Creator of all we know reached out to its Creation? But I am getting ahead of myself.

SECTION 2

WHAT DOES IT MEAN

Chapter 2

Contact

Dios, Él quien todo el mundo conoce, por
nombre. Jules Renard, Journal, (April 1894),
tr. Elizabeth Roget (English),
tr. Justin Morgan (Spanish).

God, he whom everyone knows, by name.
Jules Renard, Journal, (April 1894),
— tr Elizabeth Roget.

RETURNING TO COLLEGE WAS LIKE RUNNING INTO AN OLD
friend. It was a little awkward at first, but then we quickly
picked up right where we left off. Contrary to the warnings
I had received from well-intentioned family and friends,
resuming my studies were more a delight than a task. It was
during the five years we spent in Tennessee I was able to
broaden my worldview, mostly through the study of history. It became plain to see that throughout all of history,
Man (and Woman) have always been aware of an intelligent
creator, and probably more accurately, is still searching for
a connection to that force. Each of us has a piece of that
energy within us. It has always been apparent that, despite
similarities, we were very different from the rest of Creation.
That is to use an anthropomorphic term. This uniqueness
longs for its source, or Father. The persistent presence of
spiritualism is observed in every culture, across all corners of
the world, and into every chapter of time marks an outward
expression of an inward desire to reconnect with the source
of *our collective being.*

Have you noticed that in nature, there seems to be a tendency for similar things to gather unto their own? The water cycle is an example that demonstrates what I mean; rain collects into puddles; because of the influence of gravity, these puddles gather to form streams that form lakes and ponds, and finally, rivers flowing out to sea where by way of evaporation gather again into the clouds. Many systems, even among people, demonstrate this tendency. Immigrants disperse from all over the world into the United States and gather into puddles or ponds called ethnic communities, diaspora, or enclaves until, eventually, later generations assimilate into the general population once they become more assimilated. Perhaps this creative force or energy *does* want to interact with its Creation. Why put a homing signal in your Creation unless you wanted it to come home? There was an article in Time magazine about the discovery of a gene in humans dubbed the God gene, which prompts us to seek God.[1] I am not convinced there is an actual gene like this; however, there does seem to be something in us which keeps us looking.

I had taken three steps. There was nothing, and then there was something, but I found no explanation. Next, there was humanity, and all roads led back to where I began. There was no Man, and then there was a man (and a woman.) Thirdly, I observed that throughout recorded history, Homo sapiens had attempted to contact their Creator and find meaning or purpose in life. It seemed to me that the fourth step to take would be an investigation into whether the source of everything had attempted to made contact.

Over the next several years, I engaged myself in an extensive study of history searching for evidence of supernatural contact. At the beginning of this search, I did not restrain my focus to any time or geographic location or a specific group of people. I was careful to study only valid records or what some call 'contextually accurate property,' verified by external and internal evidence. With astonishment, it became clear that there is very little evidence of any kind concerning all ancient civilizations. I listened to expert's claims that there are treasure troves of artifacts and manuscripts documenting the ancient world. Further stated, modern Man has nearly complete knowledge of these things. However, this is not the case. Our understanding is cursory at best with one extraordinary exception. Because of voluminous surviving written documentation[2], and an atypical number of surviving artifacts and other archeological evidence, we have extensive knowledge of ancient Hebrew history. A large portion of what we know about ancient peoples came by the close study of Hebrew literature. Virtually all archeological discoveries have only further confirmed the accuracy of both the Old and New Testaments, according to an article in Time magazine.[3] Any refuting evidence does not exist. Recently there was a discovery of a 15th century B.C. Egyptian chariot wheels at the bottom of the Red Sea which is consistent with the Bible's documentation of Moses parting the Red Sea and the ensuing chase by Pharaoh Rameses II army.[4] (Bible, Exodus chapter 14, verses 21 – 31).

The Torah (also known as the Tanakh or Mikra or Old Testament) is one of the wealthiest and most authoritative sources of historical information concerning the origins of human beings by professional academic historians of many different persuasions.[5] Even historians researching other cultures commonly regard the Torah as a precious resource for accurate material. Much of the American justice system has at its roots the Torah.[6] The Jews (Hebrews were known as Jews beginning around the sixth century B.C.) had a subset of their population known as the Scribes whose sole vocation was the meticulous copying of ancient writings and documenting many details of daily living. But I am getting ahead of myself.

Chapter 3

The Bible

Elegimos un texto aquí y allá para hacerlo funcionar con nuestros propósitos; sin embargo, si tomamos en cuenta todo el texto junto y consideramos lo que pasó antes y después, descubriríamos que no significa nada así.
— John Selden, "The Scriptures,"
Table Talk (1689).

We Pick out a text here and there to make it serve our turn; whereas, if we take it all together, and considered what went before and what followed after, we should find it meant no such thing.
— John Selden, "The Scriptures,"
Table Talk (1689).

THE FIRST BOOK OF SIGNIFICANCE PRINTED on GUTENBERG'S newly invented printing press (1454 AD) was The Holy Bible.[1] The Bible is the best-selling and most widely distributed book circulating an estimated 6 billion copies.[2] "If every Bible in any considerable city were to be destroyed, the book could be restored in all its essential parts from quotations from other books on the shelves of the City Public Library." [3] "No other book has been so chopped, knifed, sifted, scrutinized, and vilified. What book on philosophy or religion or psychology has been subject to such a mass attack as the Bible? With such venom and skepticism? With such thoroughness and erudition? Upon every chapter, line, and tenet?

And yet, the Bible is still loved by millions, read by millions, and studied by millions." [4]

I found this riveting. I was beginning to become impressed with the credentials of the Holy Bible, and I decided to dig a little deeper into how well-authenticated this thirty-five hundred-year-old book was. The New Testament written between A.D.48 and A.D. 95 is the most documented work from antiquity supported by 24,686 manuscripts dated within less than 100 years of the original writings. Homer's Iliad (eighth century B.C.), is the second best-documented ancient work. Six hundred forty-three surviving manuscripts are originating within 500 years of the original.[5] Up to this point, the Bible seems unique, but is it supernatural?

Addressing hundreds of controversial subjects and written over an approximant 1600-year time span by 40 distinct authors from all walks of life such as kings, peasants, political leaders, fishers, etc., the Bible was written in three languages on three continents. Despite its incredible journey, it retains perfect continuity and consistency throughout. This consistency flies in the face of so-called experts who deceitfully claim that the biblical text suffers from inconsistencies. It is simply untrue. Further, the scientific accuracy of the textual content was far beyond the human race's general and scientific knowledge for the entire period of its origin. For example, in the scripture, a sphere that hangs on nothing is a description of Earth. It also speaks of ocean currents called paths and freshwater springs in the sea.

Further, the Bible discusses water cycles and jet streams. One author even mentions that the life of Man is in his blood. I found that very interesting as I recall that bloodletting was a standard health treatment in the not too distant past. The Bible was thousands of years ahead of its time in its knowledge of the natural world. Another point to consider is the accuracy of recorded prophesies, such as the rise and fall of kingdoms and nations, which came to pass hundreds of years later, precisely as foretold. I was slowly beginning to agree with others who considered this work to be of supernatural origin.

I discovered that the Bible has not always been such a popular book. It has survived several serious attempts to abolish it entirely from the face of the Earth. The Catholic Church tried to pollute the canonized Bible. In 1546 at the Council of Trent, the Catholics canonized an additional 19 apocryphal books to the Old Testament[6] and authorized another 27 apocryphal books to the New Testament.[7] These 46 books were all written after the death of the apostles[8]. What exactly *were* the requirements of a book to be admitted to the canon?

Curiously, it is difficult to determine which standards and methods the members of this Council used to decide which books to include in the New Testament. Though they left us a list of 27 books recognized as authoritative, they did not leave the list of criteria that they used to make this list.

Nevertheless, most scholars agree to the use of the following six tests during authentication.[9]

1) Did a prophet or apostle write it?
2) An associate of a prophet or apostle writes it.
3) Truthfulness.
4) Is the text faithful to previously accepted canonical writings?
5) Christ, prophet or apostle confirms it.
6) Church usage and recognition.

With an eye toward evidence of contact, I set out to survey the Holy Bible, beginning with the Old Testament. I did not intend to, nor do I claim to have produced any scholarly work. I decided for my purpose; I would make an informal cursory examination of the literature.

The Old Testament is divided into sections like history, law, and the prophecy of a *Messiah* (Hebrew word for anointed), to establish a new kingdom and other topics such as poetry and wisdom. The New Testament is also divided into sections called the Gospels (life of the Christ), history, and letters that end with the Revelation, which is a book of prophecy. Some say the revelations of Revelations found fulfillment in the first century A.D.; others say the foretellings have yet to find satisfaction in these modern times.

To my utter delight, the first few pages of the first book of the Old Testament titled Genesis provided many answers to some of my most pressing questions. In a few minutes of reading, I learned the origins of the cosmos, our world, and of Man (and Woman). My theory of contact between Creator and Creation stood validated. Nevertheless, what did this all mean in practical terms? It took me several months of study to obtain an idea of what the Old Testament was all about, but here goes the gist.

God made the world and everything in the world, including a man named Adam and a woman named Eve. The world was a beautiful place, and living was comfortable. Adam and Eve did not wear any clothes because there was no need to; there was no such thing as badness, shame, or anything negative. It seems in these early days God was in the habit of visiting them regularly. He told them they could eat of any tree in his garden except for one called the tree of the knowledge of good and evil; keep in mind how important it is to understand there is no love unless there is a choice to reject. Of course, they went and ate the fruit of that one forbidden tree, which angered God. Disobedience was the introduction of sin into the world and satan's bid for the rule of God's Earth. Sin is disobeying a law that God made. The penalty for such transgression is death. The punishment seems harsh, but God tells them if they sacrifice the life of a specified animal, he would overlook their sin; not fulfilling the penalty for sin would kind of be like getting out on bail. Thus humanity's schooling on the economy of sin.

At the time of Noah and his family (about 1,650 years later), the world's population of humans had only evil thoughts in their hearts, and God decided to wipe them, and all other animals off the face of the Earth, because they had grieved him. However, Noah and his family found favor in God's eyes because he had "walked" with God. God destroyed the Earth and everything on the planet by The Great Flood, save for Noah's family and the animals they had saved in their ark. I found it fascinating to discover there are more than 500 documented ancient stories of such flood in nearly every contemporaneous culture.[10] God had given a second chance for His Creation.

[One thing which puzzled me was there are three distinct lines in humanity's family tree.
If we came from Adam and Eve, would not the family tree have only one root? According to the experts, there are three lines of humanity: Occidental, Oriental, and Mongoloid. All races of modern men fall into one of these classifications. I found a possible explanation in the account of the flood. After the destruction of all life on Earth by water, Noah's three sons and their wives began a new family tree with three trunks.
Even though our family tree has three trunks, there is still one root since Noah's three sons descended from Adam and Eve. (It's a theory or more accurately just a thought.)]

About 425 years later, God called one man named Abram (descended from Noah's son Shem) to follow Him. God said, "I will make you into a great nation. I will bless you and make you famous, and you will be a blessing to others. I will bless those who bless you and curse those who treat you with contempt. All the families on Earth will be blessed through you." (Bible, Genesis chapter 12, verses 2 and 3.) The Israelites legacy begins (about 1916 B.C.).

God made a promise to Abram. "So Abram settled in the land of Canaan, and Lot moved his tents to a place near Sodom and settled among the cities of the plain. I am giving all this land, as far as you can see, to you and your descendants as a permanent possession." (Bible, Genesis, chapter 13, verses 12 and 15.); note that God changed Abram's name to Abraham in Genesis, chapter 17, verse 5. Over the next 1,946 years or so, God tries to lead the descendants of Abraham; sometimes it worked, and sometimes it did not. Several pivotal moments changed the direction of this sacred family.

In 1701 BC, about 640 years after the end of the "Great Flood," Jacob, who was later called Israel, moved his family to Egypt as the guest of the Pharaoh Apachman because of a 7-year famine. In return, Israel and his family tended to the Pharaoh's livestock. This visit lasted about 126 years, and then a new Pharaoh named Amosis decided that all of Israel's family would become slaves (side note: if you overstay your welcome, your host *may* get a little grumpy). In the next couple of hundred years, this chosen family lived in slavery. God helped to get them out of that jam calling Moses to lead his people across the Red Sea on dry ground but talk about jumping out of the frying pan into another fire. The people of Israel had lived in Egypt for 430 years (Bible, Exodus chapter 12, verse 40). Even spending the next 40 years wandering in the wilderness and receiving the Ten Commandments from God's mouth and written by his hand didn't seem to do the trick. When they took possession of the Promised Land, they apparently could only endure a few years being faithful to their God, before beginning to incorporate other religions. Regular as clockwork, they would be good for 7 to 40 years, and then they would drift away, and "The Israelites did evil in the Lord's sight. So, the Lord handed them over to the Midianites for seven years." (Bible, Judges chapter 6, verse 1). God would then allow a surrounding nation to overrun and enslave the Israelites for 20 years or so. Then they would repent, and He would restore their land to them yet again. After about 368 years of living under the God-approved "Judges form of rule" and repeating the AODD pattern (Apostasy, Oppression, Distress, and then Deliverance), the Israelites decided they wanted a new form of government. They wanted a *king*, like their neighboring countries. Although they rejected the leadership of God, He complied with their wishes. God gave them kings. Some were good, and some were bad. After about 108 years under royal rule, Israel split into two kingdoms Israel and Judah. The Assyrians captured Israel about 229 years later. Nearly 97 years downstream, the Babylonians began exiling these Jews to various parts of their empire. Israel would never be an independent kingdom again (however, in 1947 A.D., the re-established Israel repatriated by Jews from all over the world has to date never enjoyed peace.) Babylonians were the first to call the descendants of Abraham "Jews". The next oppressors in line were the Greeks and then the Romans.

[I would like to interject a thought at this point. From the Great Deluge to the birth of Jesus, what was going on with the rest of the world's inhabitants? In the Bible, we can learn of Abraham's dynasty, but what of the rest of humanity that was collectively called the "Gentiles"? Noah's three sons Shem, Ham, and Japheth, started their family trees. Abraham came of

Shem's lineage, but what of the descendants of the other two? We read of some people not of Abraham's descent, like Abimelech, a king who seemed to be familiar with, and respectful of God. We also learned that Lot's daughters' illegitimate sons started great nations of their own. They, too, were from the lineage of Shem. Then comes the issues of Ishmael's (illegitimate Son of Abraham) 12 sons and their tribes. It was through this lineage Mohammed began Islam about 610AD[11]. Adherents to Islam are known as Muslims. Although they were from the linage of Abraham, they were not in the direct line of Israel to David and, therefore, not Israelites. The New Testament states that some of these Gentiles did naturally the very things that God required of Man. It would be pure conjecture to discuss God's relationship with them but very interesting, don't you think?]

Now for the time when Jesus was born. God chose Abraham's family (Israel), to receive the blessing of being a great nation in a unique God-given location. They have had it in the past, and it was enjoyable. They had grown up with stories of the old days when the family name was respected and struck fear in the hearts of their enemies. Their heritage included a time when much wealth was theirs, and worldwide they were known for their great wisdom. However, they were at the point of despair due to harassment and disrespect. Sure, most of the Jews still managed to keep a stiff upper lip; they maintained their pride and carried on with their honorable customs and traditions. A high number of them were betting that if they practiced their religion well enough, God would give them back the glory days their ancestors had so enjoyed. After all, isn't that how it had worked for the past 2000 years? Get in a bind, you straighten up, and God fixes everything. Let us also not forget the prophecy of the coming Messiah, the Savior. The Abraham family was ripe with despair and a sense of entitlement that it was time for God to get busy and give them what he had promised if they behaved as upstanding leaders.

Jesus turned out to be a disappointment to most of the Israel clan. Jesus said things like give up your wealth, and, if a Roman soldier tells you to carry his gear for a mile, carry it two miles; if someone hits you, let him or her hit you again. He spoke about all sorts of strange ideas, but he also threw in tantalizing talk of a new kingdom and a brand-new temple. The Jewish people were biding their time for many years, waiting for the Messiah to deliver them of the hedonistic Romans and restore Jerusalem to its former glory. They expected the Messiah to lead an army against their enemies, the dark forces of this world, and reclaim Canaan land.

He did not. Jesus spent most of his time speaking of love, forgiveness and showing kindness to one another. Jesus also accused some of the most righteous men of not being very virtuous. He did perform some miracles. Anyway, he got himself crossways with the priest, and that was a huge no-no.

It was a dark day when Jesus was taken and crucified on a Roman cross. His disciples and other followers were devastated. However, on the third day after the tragedy (Sunday morning, the first day of the week), He rose from His tomb, and for forty days, he spoke to his followers about the Kingdom of God, repentance, and forgiveness. He also spoke of returning to the right hand of his Father until his return, when His enemies would become a footstool for his feet; then, he ascended to Heaven. Even so, it was not until ten days later when the Holy Spirit filled the twelve apostles and they finally understood the mystery made known to men by revelation, as I have already written briefly. In reading this, then, you will be able to understand my insight into the mystery of Christ (Bible, Ephesians chapter 3, verses 3 and 4). Finally, the revelation of redemption! The Old Covenant was only a shadow of things to come and unable to take away sin. It was just for the Jews, but God had promised Abraham that all the peoples of the Earth would receive blessings through him. Now God's New Covenant was for the Jews *and* the Gentiles. It is through the Church by the perfect blood sacrifice of Jesus, and with cleansed hearts that we enter the Most Holy place and are seated with Him in the heavenly realms. The Christian's citizenship is no longer on Earth but in Heaven. Our minds are set on things *above*, not on *earthly* things. (See Appendix 3 for a list of other names of Jesus).

In about 30 years, every living creature under Heaven had heard the Gospel (good news)! Thus, our great human experiment continues. We bide our time doing good deeds, sharing our faith, encouraging one another, praising God, and living in peace and love until Jesus the *Christ* (Greek word for anointed) returns. The righteous will change in the twinkling of an eye, and we will meet him in the air. The world and all those in the heavenly realms will witness the destruction of Christ's last enemy, satan and his demons. Our Savior will then hand over the Church to his Father, and the Son will be subject to Him. We will live in Glory forever, Amen!

Even before he made the world, God loved us and chose us in Christ to be holy and without fault in his eyes. God decided in advance to adopt us into his own family by bringing us to Him through Jesus Christ. God enjoyed great pleasure in so doing (Bible, Ephesians chapter 1, verses 4 and 5). Our Father chose one family to bring the Savior into the world at His appointed time. The following 2000 years, the small nation of Israel taught Creation, the nature of God, and the requirements of sin. The plans remained hidden until the day of Pentecost when it was revealed. Since sin requires a blood sacrifice, Jesus freely offered himself as the price for the complete redemption of all humans who obeyed the Lord, both the Jews and the Gentile (non-Jew). It is now through the Church that the wisdom of God is to be made known to all. The Church, the body of the Messiah, the Kingdom of God, and the bride of Christ, consists of believers. Believers who patiently await the day when all those in the world and heavenly places, witness the Christ's final victory over his enemy. Then He will hand the Church over to God. But I am getting ahead of myself.

Chapter 4

Jesus

Empecé al principio de todo y llegué a conocer
el Creador de todo que conocemos.
— Papá.

I began at the beginning of everything and
discovered the Creator of all we know.
— Dad.

AT THIS POINT, I REMIND YOU TERA THAT MY PURPOSE IN writing you this letter is to share with you all I have learned of significance, about life on our third rock from the sun. I have concluded this; that our Creator desired contact with His unique Creation of Mankind. I arrived at this conclusion because of an apparent drive in Mankind to connect with Him. I call this drive a homing signal; others have called it a God gene. I have shared my journey of discovering the discovery of possible points of contact with the Creator. I searched through old books and found one which is beyond comparison to any other volume known to Man. I shared with you its contents, which dealt with the origins of the cosmos, Earth, and humanity. It also revealed the sources of all races and languages.

Further, it demonstrates how the Creator who calls Himself "I Am that I Am" chose a people called the Israelites to teach the world about who He is and what He requires of us. He specifically addressed our fallibility and then laid out his plan of how to overcome that obstacle toward a real connection, because of His perfect nature. In the New

Testament, we meet a man named Jesus, who claimed to be the very Son of God. If this were the Creator's being, then it would fit with my little theory; I suspected that if the Creator wanted to contact us, he would do so in speech or writing since that is how *we* communicate. But if he came to Earth, it would be in the form of a man just like us, with a piece of the Creator in him like us, except he would be *full* of the Creator. Jesus claimed precisely that. Either he is the Son of the Creator, or he is a liar; there are no other choices. Now I will share with you my darling, my research into this matter.

I don't want to pretend to understand everything that I have discovered. I am like Christopher Columbus, who made an extraordinary discovery, but, I as he, was not fully aware of what we found. I am willing to appear as a fool for honesty. Dads are good at that - acting the fool while thinking we're cool, right? You think I am off on a tangent again, don't you? Well, for your information, I am right on track, thank you very much! I think the best place to begin my analysis of Jesus is within the pages of the most reliable book of all, the Bible. If you take the entire Bible as one piece of work, it tells an entirely coherent story. This story is about us and our shortcomings, which separate us from the Creator. More specifically, the New Testament speaks of the Creator's plan to reconcile us to Him. It seems barbaric to my sensitivities, but the Creator sent his only Son to die an innocent death, at the hands of humankind on Earth. The Creator's requirement to repair the separation between Man and Him was satisfied. I don't know about you, but that touches me somewhere deep down. I feel a twinge and a tingling inside. I do not understand it, though. The Bible states that Jesus claimed to be the Son of God, and he performed miracles, sacrificing himself on a cross and then rising from the grave. Wow, this is *way* out there. I decided to see if other non-Christian historians recorded these things, and I was not disappointed.

I found two ancient books called <u>The History of the Jewish War</u> and <u>Jewish Antiquities</u>[1] written by a Jewish historian named Flavius Josephus[1]. In his records, he spoke of one Jewish peasant who worked wonders and had amassed a following. He went on to say that the Jewish peasant, Jesus, was crucified on a Roman cross, after which he appeared to many people after his resurrection. Again, I found some of the same events in a work about Nero, written by the Roman historian Carius Cornelius Tacitus.[2] Another Roman historian Suetonius wrote a book entitled <u>The Twelve Caesars</u>,[3] in which he refers to a new religious sect called Christians. When Emperor Trajan sent Pliny the Younger to Bithynia in 112 AD, Pliny wrote back requesting information concerning on how to deal with the Christians, as they would not curse Christ or worship Trajan's image or statues of other deities. Even the Jews who hated Jesus offered corroborating details in their Babylonian Talmud.

I found this very interesting; Jews recorded the hanging of Yeshua (Hebrew for Jesus) that occurred on the eve of Passover (Friday evening). They also tell of a herald crying out for forty days prior, "He is going forth to be stoned because he has practiced sorcery and enticed Israel to apostasy," a charge He heard often. Finally, in a second-century work entitled <u>The Death of Peregrine</u>[4], the Greek satirist Lucian of Samosata makes mention of the Christians. They think of themselves as brothers refusing to worship the Grecian gods to the point of death. It became clear to me in light of this collateral documentation that once again, the Bible is proven to be a reliable source of information. And Jesus is the Son of God who was born of a virgin named Mary and grew up to preach, performing many miracles and signs and was crucified on a Roman cross only to rise on the third day (Sunday morning). Further, the documentation says he left an empty tomb and made appearances for forty days to many people, after which he ascended to Heaven, promising to return one day. This stuff is so exciting and interesting, but where do I go from here?

My journey has been a long and eventful one. I have learned of the origins of the planets and stars, I have learned of the origins of all life here on *la Tierra Firma*, I have learned the history of Man, and I have learned that the name of the Creator is "I Am that I Am," (see more names of God in appendix #2). I have learned that the Bible is reliable. I have also learned of God's requirements of us. Moreover, I have learned of His generous provisions to meet these requirements. What does all this mean to me? What does all this say to us, and what do we do now? Further, what implication does this have after we pass from this life if any? But I am getting ahead of myself.

Chapter 5

The Church

Afortunado es el hombre que se acuerda de su
niñez con cariño
— Papá.

Fortunate is the man who remembers his
childhood with fondness
— Dad.

I WAS FORTUNATE AS A YOUNG MAN TO HAVE A PAPER ROUTE.
During my junior high school years, I was always the one
out of my peer group who had funds available for whatever
emergency arose. There were many times I averted starvation
or boredom with my fiscal preparedness. With the purchase
of my 1969 Chevy Camaro, I was able to obtain more pros-
perous employment. In high school, I worked the graveyard
shift and began classes at 7:30 a.m. I remember one morning during my Ancient History class; something startled
me. After regaining my composure, I resumed taking notes
on the lecture, but I was puzzled. Why were we discussing
the Civil War? I scanned the room, and suddenly, my face
began to flush as I realized I had slept through the passing
bell and the changing of classes. I stood, received my standing ovation from these new classmates, and then left for my
next class. I suppose Ancient History did not hold my attention very well in those days. It was a strange experience then
when decades later, I found myself researching historical
sites on the Web and historical works in the library looking
for roots of various world religions. I remember thinking as

a rebellious young man, "when will I ever need to know who these dead men were or what they did?" Who knew what was in store for me?

I searched through the documents of many world religions and found many dead men, but I will get back to that later. I had a burning question, "What am I to do with all I have learned?" Had I found the connection people had been waiting for, or should I continue my search? Perhaps I would find the answer in religion or some other system of belief. I have always been fascinated with the splendor of some religions and the mystery of others. I had the opportunity to peek into all those beautiful sanctuaries I had seen all over the world. There are thousands of religions in the world; however, they fall into just a few categories. Some of these religions frightened me as I began to study them. Mostly, these religions seemed to concern themselves with some moral code of conduct. Only Christianity (33 A.D.) actively seeks an intimate connection between the Creator and the created. To put it succinctly, none of the great religions of the world were even of the same caliber as Christianity. Christianity is more of a reconciled relationship than a religion. Notice I did not say Christianity is not a religion because it is a religion. Christianity is a belief system plus; only within the Christian faith alone are all the needs in all areas of life met for humans.

Man is a unique creation because God created him in his image. The created Man has a purpose, and each life has its objective. Other belief systems do not bear this out. These other belief systems led to social movements like Communism and Hitler's Nazism. In Christianity, there is a significant emphasis on the dignified and respectful treatment of all Earth inhabitants. Christ has commanded us to live a peaceful and quiet life turning the cheek when treated poorly and going the extra mile when called upon to serve. It was The Christian Church that instituted the first hospitals and universities. It was stressed to love and pray for your enemies.

Mohammed advocated murder if done for religious purposes, and even promised special blessings to the slayer. The reincarnation religions like Hinduism view the accidental death as fate, and if an individual intervened to prevent an accident, the well-intentioned rescuer earned chastisement. Mahatma Gandhi said, "Of all the dispositions and teachings of thinkers and ethicists, the one doctrine that I have no sufficient counter for is Jesus on that Cross." [1] Many of these religions, including Buddhism, seem to have little regard for the rights or needs of women. In several instances, women have no chance to receive a reward for a life of faithful adherence to their system of belief, or hope for a better life. Further, while men's sexual needs are stressed as the Woman's responsibility, there are no provisions for meeting her needs.

Within the Christian faith, sex between a husband and wife is a gift from God. Physical intimacy is intended for mutual pleasure as well as for procreation. The sensual nature of sex creates a bond that is an exclusive relationship not found in any other relationship. The symbolism of marriage constructs a compelling word picture for God's love of his people and the Church. (Song of Solomon, Hosea, Ezekiel 16, Ephesians 5:22-33, Revelations 21:2.) Indeed, the Bible paints a unique picture of human passion.

Man is the head of the Woman (Our Father created the female from the man for man), but both men and women are to submit to each other. The man is explicitly commanded to love his wife as he loves himself, and the Woman is expressly commanded to respect her husband. Several of the Eastern religions take children out of the home during their early years to teach them their belief system. Children are told to be obedient, and parents instructed to discipline them, sometimes harshly. The New Testament instructs children to obey their parents, and it tells fathers explicitly not to exasperate their children, or they will become discouraged. Parents are advised to teach their children's hearts and not to break their spirits. The Bible directs Man to till the soil and exercise dominion over all the animals, to inhabit all the Earth and subdue it, and to manage them well. It says that plants and animals are suitable for food. Other religions don't farm or eat meat, and this has caused them difficulties. The Christian way is very different. Biblical teachings are unique among all other religions.

The Christian faith is a religion plus: it is a system of belief *and* relationships. It is a personal relationship with God, Jesus, and the Holy Spirit (the Holy Spirit is another conversation we shall have later.) It is a family relationship with fellow believers. Also, it is the only religion that assures your salvation and reward at the moment of your acceptance. It is indeed the only religion that offers peace and joy *in the here and now.*

If I were to design a model of how I would think the source of this created world would want us to interact with each other and the planet, and the desire it would have to connect with us, I would envision something like The Christian faith. However, two things I did not expect to find. One that the Creator would be so explicit in declaring his love for us creatures, and second, his offer of reconnecting with him would require nothing of us except our response. But I am getting ahead of myself.

Chapter 6

Rites, Rituals, and Traditions

Misteriosos son los ritos hechos detrás de la tela
negra y ventanas de vitral del santuario y a
qué fin me pregunto.
— Papá.

Mysterious are the rituals performed behind
the black cloth and stained-glass windows of
the sanctuary and for what purpose I wonder.
— Dad.

WE WALKED QUIETLY AND RESPECTFULLY DOWN THE AISLE toward an elegant wooden box. The five of us were cousins, and our solidarity emboldened our actions. I wondered why there was a table with so many candles burning left unattended. We approached the oak box and eyed a slotted opening in the lid, which begged the question who was going to stick their hand down there into the box and discover its secrets? After a few moments of quiet bickering, it fell to me to be the one who would dare defile this sacred article. I slowly and cautiously slid my hand deeper and deeper into the box, terrified of what I might find until I reached the spongy bottom. The unexpected texture gave me such a start that I let out a squeal as I bluntly retracted my hand. It was not until a few moments later; I realized I had several slicing cuts to the back of my hand. The mysterious box was a collection box with a device that discouraged individuals from making unauthorized withdrawals.

Sometimes when I reminisce over my previous years, I am dumbfounded that I was capable of such foolish behavior. I shared this little piece of my history to illustrate my awe and ignorance of the sacred. I have always been fascinated by the magnificent beauty of massive church buildings. Like a kid in the candy store or like a little one waiting up for Santa Clause, the majesty of the great-spired houses of worship elicited great awe. However, it was always with a sense of foreboding that I would approach these structures for a closer inspection. Then I would wonder, where did all the money come from to build such an expensive house, and why would anyone go to such trouble? Why did some of these buildings have bell towers? What is the purpose of the stained-glass windows? The whole idea of religious architecture, art, and even music seemed to me to be a secret culture. I set out to lift the black cloth and peer through the stained glass to discover the hidden mysteries.

Since the beginning, the Church has sung. Singing is in all times and all cultures throughout history. What cannot be adequately expressed in writing or words can exquisitely be communicated through song. Music is the language of our souls. It is a part of daily life, celebrations, and worship. Because the Christian faith arose from Judaism, (more precisely, Christianity is the requirements of Judaism fulfilled), it is not surprising that the early Church (the word Church means the assembly or the called out) also used the Psalms for their musical worship. Talented early Christians began to write new arrangements of the Psalms and other traditional music. Unfortunately, the well-intentioned musicians in their efforts to offer their best work created music too complicated for the ordinary vocalist to execute. The ensuing garbled performances were deemed unacceptable, and the idea for choral music was born. It was not until hundreds of years after the beginning of the Church that song lyrics other than Old Testament scripture began to appear in congregational singing, and the same is true of its instrumental accompaniment. These new songs were religious themes set to modern tunes. I cannot help but remember my grandparents' shock and disgust when in the early 1970s, some young Christians began adapting Christian music to contemporary folk music. I feel confident the idea of modernizing musical worship in the 800's must have met with the same resistance! Is it not odd what my grandparents thought appropriate music (music written from the 1600s to the 1940s), was indeed scandalous at its introduction? And what I consider appropriate, you probably would think is ancient history? Perhaps the study of history is of some value. I do believe that some music is timeless.

Why is music such a big deal in churches? Some churches still sing those old songs from the Isaac Watts era, and others sing very modern music. Some churches have choirs, and others sing as a congregation. Some churches sing a cappella while others opt for instrumental accompaniment. What I discovered is that music is a part of worship. That statement may sound trite at first; however, it struck me as profound. My perception of religious music was that it is enjoyable, and it encourages, and I still think that is the case. However, I was surprised to learn another reason these people are singing is they are offering a sacrificial gift to God. There are not many things we can give God, but this is one thing anyone, even a tone-deaf mutant like me, can give to God. Real worship is giving gifts to God.

The idea of giving a gift to God seems inconceivable. How can a little human soul provide the Creator of everything and anything? I guess the answer is worship. Whenever I think of the word "Worship," I imagine someone bowing down in front of a king or something similar, but that is too narrow a definition. Another gift we can give our Father and is a ritual called contribution or simply *giving*. The giving of finances or possessions is a familiar idea but not very well understood, or I should say I did not have an accurate understanding of this in my younger days. It seems silly now, but I used to think the contribution was the preacher's pay, which was why he preached so intently. The better he preached, the more his remuneration. It was a perfectly reasonable assumption. Of course, that is not the way it works, but to a child, it made sense.

Giving money is part of our worship; another more modern word is honoring. These funds pay the church staff, including the minister, administrative assistants, counselors, and church building expenses and all different kinds of supplies. I would be remiss if I did not include the donated monies support missionaries and fund local benevolence work too. The idea of tithing is a carryover from the Old Testament and the Jewish religion (Judaism.) This idea refers to the practice of giving a tenth of one's possessions, both financial and material, to God as he instructed. These funds paid the priest, funded temple construction, and benevolence activities. Does this sound familiar? In the New Testament, giving is a little different.

The New Testament records the life of Jesus, the very early history of the Church, and some letters written to various congregations and individuals and one letter of Revelation. All these written by Apostles and probably by two of his brothers, James and Jude. Jesus chose 12 apostles from among his disciples. In the very early Church, Christians met in each other's homes, barns, or just about anywhere there was room, and sometimes because of vigorous persecution, safety from being discovered was a chief concern. Therefore, church buildings did not exist. We read of gathered collections sent to other groups of Christians who had a great need because of the persecution. Apostles who were traveling from city to city and country-to-country preaching the Good News also received gifts of collections. Several letters to various Churches instructed them to take up offerings and praised their generosity. At other times the Apostles would earn their living so as not to be a burden to the local congregation.

Presently, many congregations take up collections each week, and while the New Testament never mentions an exact amount to give. Many Christians seem to donate ten percent of their income routinely, and they offer even more when special needs arise. I am surprised at the number of hospitals and universities supported by Christians. There are many things in society we take for granted. But that is another story for another time. Another Christian ritual that required many years to understand and appreciate was prayer.

It was you and your brothers that taught me a lot about praying. At first, I wondered if it was appropriate, praying for ladybugs, but I learned as time went on. Your Mother and I taught each of you how to pray in the traditional ways. On our knees with our hands pressed together and our heads bowed. We prayed for the day and the day's activities. We prayed for your brothers and for your grandparents too. As you got older, your prayers became longer and filled with surprises. I learned a lot about what was going on in that little head of yours by listening to your prayers, and I learned prayer is for every part of our life, not just the churchy stuff. I remember it like it was yesterday. You were five years old, and you had just finished your bath before bedtime. You ran across our polished wooden floor in the living room and leaped into the couch in front of a huge picture window. Do they still call big windows picture windows? Anyway, as you so enthusiastically jumped up and down on the sofa, you casually asked, "If God is good and He lives in us, how can we do bad things?" I was a 26-year-old Bible student at a private University, and you floored me! Tera, to this day, I still cannot answer that question adequately, but I am always searching. Out of the mouth of babes!

Getting back to prayer, I will mention several things. Consider all the religions of the world and even a few scientific theories if you like. Which ones adequately explain the origins of all that exists, offer a reasonable and coherent answer to the meaning of life question, provide a logical and functional code of ethics, and even previews our up comings as the British say? Christianity! Right! However, I am biased, and I already know that. So, what is my point? No point, just an awkward segue to this. Only in Christian prayer, does the creature directly approach the Creator and make a request. There is more to prayer than making a solicitation. When the disciples of Jesus asked Him to teach them how to pray, he prayed what is known as the Lord's Prayer.

Pray like this:

Our Father in Heaven,
may your name be kept holy.
May your Kingdom come soon.
May your will be done on Earth,
as it is in Heaven.
Give us today the food we need,
and forgive us our sins,
as we have forgiven those who sin against us.
And don't let us yield to temptation,
but rescue us from the evil one.
(Bible, Matthew chapter 6, verses 9-13 and
Luke chapter 11, verses 1-4.)

There have been many discussions about prayer in the Church. Should one bow their head when praying? Perhaps when approaching God, one should bend their knee. Better yet, when approaching the Almighty, one should lie flat on their face and dare not look up! I do not intend any disrespect, so let me further illustrate my message. How is it that the Creator of this world has not created millions and millions of other planets like this one? If he has, we do not know of it, at least not yet! Why is it that the Creator of everything is interested in us? Hold that thought in your mind. I have visited many different churches and other social and even civic gatherings where entire groups of us unkempt and uncouth commoners were invited to speak with the God of Heaven. What kind of God is He? The type that does not mind rolling up his sleeves and getting his hands dirty? That's a good thing because we can sure get dirty down here trying to scratch our way through life. I know I have some stains of which I am not so proud. You know me, Tera. We all have blemishes. It indeed is a fantastic thing that we can let our requests be made known to God, he hears, he cares, and he answers. We can pray anytime, and we can pray anywhere. The line is never busy, and he is always there. Sometimes I pray while driving down the road. Sometimes I pray immediately when one of your brothers tells me he wrecked the car. He is always there ready to listen and to help. Stop and think for a minute. You hear people praying all the time all around you. It does not matter where you go you will hear, "Oh my God!" or maybe, "Oh God!" or even when people are frustrated with how He does things you will hear, "God damn it!" Everyone knows that He is right here, and in emergencies, and He is the only one who can help. They know He is the giver of all good things, and sadly, they blame him when satan screws things up!

Another Christian ritual that bears investigation is that of Baptism. I am struck again that such an ancient behavior exists currently, and yet upon further study, I have learned that this aspect of (which is our spirituality) is timeless. Spiritual truths of a thousand years ago are the same today as they were at their inception. The word Baptism is a transliterated one, which means that instead of being translated into English, it retains its similar Greek form. Baptisma or Baptismo translated directly means immersed. I suspect out of a sense of respect for this sacred institution, it remains in original manuscript form. Or perhaps it was fear of King James, who was baptized by sprinkling that inhibited the translators' work.

The New Testament relates that at Jesus' Baptism or Immersion, the Spirit descended upon him like a dove, and God said, "This is my son in whom I am well pleased." Later the apostles instruct those to whom they preach to "Repent of their sins and to be baptized for the remission of their sins." Within the Christian community (217 denominations in the USA, 350,000 congregations nearly all of which believe in Baptism in one form or another.)[1], there has been much discussion about what Baptism is or, what does it accomplish. But regardless of the studies, the consensus seems to be that Baptism is something which repentant believers in Christ do to become Christians. I think there are differing opinions on when you become a Christian, either before or after being baptized. Still, it seems everyone agrees that to be a Christian, you must believe the teachings of the Christ and repent of wrongdoings and make a commitment to God and do whatever He asked. That is my take on it. To be clear, several out-lying Christian religions do not practice Baptism, but that is a whole other study.

The most recognized Christian ritual is probably the wedding ceremony. About 63% of the marriages in this country are religious ceremonies. However, a downward trend is becoming apparent.[2] This land has a deep sense of tradition concerning marriage. The heavy influence of religious rites has impacted the culture of our country. Christians consider marriage a sacred institution and a spiritual experience.

Conversely, in days past, only the Church granted divorces, but now a civil institution may grant a divorce. Viewed as an inconsistent turn of events, but it is how things have evolved. I hope that you will never have to suffer through such unfortunate incidents.

Darling, if you decide to go exploring churches, there are a few things for which you should prepare yourself. Speaking strictly from an anthropological point of view, churches are a subculture that adheres to numerous subtle rules and traditions, customs, and even codified language or jargon. Be prepared to be greeted by unusually enthusiastic individuals who will most likely shake your hand vigorously as if you are a VIP, or maybe it is as if they are an important person. It is usually an authentic attempt to be friendly. They may or may not refer to themselves and others as brothers and sisters; however, this does not indicate blood relations; instead, they are terms of endearment. Do not become bewildered when you hear phraseology with which you are unfamiliar; this is not necessarily indicative of cultic behavior. Understand, you entered a group that belongs to an organization that evolved over many centuries with an emphasis on *not* being affected by the secular world. Toto, we are not in Kansas anymore!

Finally, the last ceremony to discuss here is communion. As is par for this course, we call it a religious ritual; there are several opinions concerning the appropriate observance of this rite. First, let us consider a bit of background history on the origins of this custom. Like other Christian traditions, this ritual has its roots in Jewish tradition. Jesus observed the Passover feast with his disciples' just hours before his crucifixion on the Roman cross. It was not well understood at this time that Jesus was instituting a new tradition. However, in later writings, the Apostles and Christians are instructed to observe this memorial regularly, recollecting Jesus' death and its sacrificial implications. Communion is now a Christian ritual modeled after a Jewish ceremony or tradition.

Currently, the observance of the "Lord's Supper" is on the first day of the week and consists of partaking of unleavened bread and the "fruit of the vine," which is historically grape juice or wine. The correct performance of this rite has been the subject of considerable discussion for many years within the Christian community. Specifics as to how many cups to use or the appropriate presentation of the unleavened bread, who shall preside over the administration and what is the proper frequency of observation foolishly remains a point of contention among a very few. I think everyone should determine for himself or herself what is pleasing to our Father. I think it would be so regrettable if one were to take this circumstance and label it sin because others disagree agree with their preferences. But I am getting ahead of myself.

SECTION 3

HOW DO I LIVE

UTILITIES

Chapter 7

Sin and satan

Escucha a la historia del tiempo del Hombre.
— Papá.

Listen to the story of Man's time.
— Dad.

GOD PLACED ADAM AND EVE IN THE GARDEN OF EDEN AND instructed them to care for the plants and eating the fruit of every tree except one in the middle of the garden called the Tree of the Knowledge of Good and Evil. As you probably already know, the serpent came to speak to Eve, and he enticed her to look at the fruit of the forbidden tree and to see that it was pleasing to the eye and that it was desirable for gaining wisdom. He lied to her and said that when you eat from the tree, "you will not surely die." He also told her a part of the truth "that when you eat of it, your eyes will be opened, and you will be like God, knowing good and evil." She gave some to her husband. When God next spoke to them, he told the woman,

Then he said to the woman,
"I will sharpen the pain of your pregnancy,
and in pain, you will give birth.
And you will desire to control your husband,
but he will rule over you."
And to the man he said,
"Since you listened to your wife and ate from the tree
whose fruit I commanded you not to eat,

the ground is cursed because of you.
All your life, you will struggle to scratch a living from it.
It will grow thorns and thistles for you,
though you will eat of its grains.
By the sweat of your brow
will you have food to eat
until you return to the ground
from which you were made.
For you were made from dust,
and to dust, you will return."
(Bible, Genesis chapter 3, verses 16-19.)

Sin entered the world and affected some of its folks and the Earth itself. I suspect that before the introduction of sin, the world was a very different place. Earth was a place with no illness or disease, a place with no aches and pains, a place with no rocks in the soil or pollution in the air. Now we must wear clothes to cover our less than perfect bodies. Work in this stained existence makes me sweat, and it is stressful. I inherited both my parents' bad genes, luckily, along with a couple of good ones. Sadly, our brothers and sisters don't get along very well; therefore, we live with the threat of war and terrorism. The old neighborhood sure has changed.

Initially, I had not planned on introducing the subjects of sin and satan; however, I feel that the contrast will vastly improve your appreciation of the other positive topics of which I have written. Sin is one of those churchy words which, with much use, has lost most of its original meaning. If I had to choose one word to describe life, I would select relationships. Life is a long series of relationships, and sin is a violation of a relationship. It is the failure to respect the dignity of another, and it is the failure to recognize the dignity of self. The Bible mentions that there are three different kinds of sin; the lust of the flesh, the lust of the eyes, and the pride of life; they all violate a relationship by failing to respect the dignity of someone. It could even be a self-relationship violation, or it could be a violation against God. To our way of thinking, there must be big sins and small sins. But, God's word states: For the person who keeps all the laws except one is as guilty as a person who has broken all of God's laws. (Bible, James chapter 2, verse 10.) All sin is a crime against God.

Similarly, the consequence of all sin is the same. It seems to us that the effects of having an impure thought and the consequences of adultery would be very dissimilar, and they are in this world, but in the spiritual realm, the results are the same. In the spirit realm, both situations would be victories for the old serpent. Both crimes are punishable by death. It is a good thing we have a spiritual credit card with no limit.

The lust of the flesh is generally a crime committed against your body. These sins seem to involve appetites or cravings, which can lead to addiction; these sins seem to be violations against the self-relationship, including the sins of gluttony, drug abuse, and illicit sexual behavior, etc. The immediate negative consequences are mostly obvious. The body will retaliate against you. Your good health will abandon your body.

The lust of the eyes is generally crimes committed outside yourself with your mind. These sins involve thoughts directed toward other people or things. These thoughts often but not necessarily lead to actions. Examples of these kinds of sin are envy, greed, and covetousness. These sins violate the relationship you have with other people. The consequences of this kind of transgression are not so obvious. They are "stinking thinking and hardening of the attitudes[1]", which lead to a bitter and angry disposition. You will not be fun to be around!

The pride of life is a crime committed against God. It is the subtlest sin and, therefore, difficult to see in others. This insidious sin can involve the body and the mind as well as your spirit. Crimes of this kind include conceit, pride, and rebellion against God's will. The violation is the abuse of your relationship with God. Specifically, it is the refusal to seek His will and instead opt to follow our own will. A person living with this kind of sin can appear to others as a righteous individual. They may be familiar with the Holy Bible and seem to have a strong relationship with Jesus and be very connected to the Church family and yet still rebel against God's will. Only our Heavenly Father can see into the hearts of men.

So why should we not sin? Because it kills us spiritually, because it separates us from God, because it hurts us, and it is a rebellion against God; to sin is to lack love. Sin is tall on promises of pleasure but short on delivery of said promises. These desires give birth to sinful actions, and when sin grows, it gives birth to death. (Bible, James chapter 1, verse 15).

Another aspect of sin is satan. Some say that our bodies are naturally sinful because they are of this earth, but that does not make sense to me. If that were true, then everything in the world would contain some element of evil, and that is not what God said when He created them. He said that *He saw that it was good*. Further, when He created man, 'He saw that it was very good.' When Adam and Eve sinned in the Garden of Eden, God said, "The man has now become like one of us, knowing good and evil." Now that sin is in the world, and now that we know good and evil, the Good Book says, "Temptation comes from our desires, which entice us and drag us away…" (Bible, James chapter 1, verse 14.) I hope you do not misunderstand this. Our bodies are not evil, and the spirit of life within us is not evil; satan is evil. If we were born evil, then we would not have free will, which would be unjust of God. He gives us the ability to choose. He knows we are weak and that we cannot live a perfect life, which is why he made the plan of His son's atonement for our sin. The influence of sin has weakened our bodies. As there are rocks and weeds in the soil, so too, there are imperfections in the flesh. Some of us have predispositions toward substance abuse, gambling, or sexual sin at the genetic level; however, we still have our free will, and we can choose our behaviors. Remember that satan and his demons are trying to manipulate us into sinning by using deceptive enticements and seduction aimed at our body, mind, and spirit.

Some of his names are the angels of the bottomless pit: antichrist, the god of this world, leviathan, murderer, prince of the devils, son of the morning, the spirit who now works in the sons of disobedience, swine, tempter and the unclean spirit. (see appendix # 4.) His only purpose is to dissuade as many people as possible from loving God. His primary goal is not to recruit followers of himself but to decrease the number of followers of our Father. Most people who think themselves to be Christians do so because they believe in God, and they believe they live kind lives. You say you have faith, for you believe that there is one God. Good for you! Even the demons believe this, and they tremble in terror. (Bible, James chapter 2, verse 19) The evil one wants to hurt God and those whom God loves. He is powerful and shrewd, but unlike our Father, he does not possess all knowledge, and he cannot be everywhere at once; he is not all-powerful. He has many demons to help him with his work.

satan and his demons are spirits like God and his angels. Therefore, the work of satan can continue unnoticed by a mortal Man quite easily and much, in the same manner, God's work can go unnoticed. These activities are occurring here on earth but in the spiritual realm out of the sight of

Man. In this realm, there is a battle raging day and night between the armies of God and satan. We are unaware participants in this drama; our daily choices to honor or dishonor our love relationships either turns the tide in favor of our Father's army or turns the tide against Him. Because we have free will, satan cannot overpower us or force us to do his will. However, he and his demons are master manipulators, efficient enticers, sultry seducers, and intrepid influencers. They know our weaknesses and love a good game of deception.

Our life is a path through a dark land, the land darkened by sin. If we were able to see the spirit realm, we would know that we are walking on a golden path, which is bright and narrow. It is also straight and level, leading off into the distance to a bright shiny city called Heaven, where our Father is waiting for us. If you glance off to either side of the path, you will see many seemingly good things like money and fame, and power and pleasure; rows and rows of tables loaded with every good food and drink; stacks and stacks of the latest and best merchandise; handsome men and beautiful women with that look in their eyes waiting for you. Off in the distance, you hear loud party music, and just beyond the rise of the land, you see bright floodlights and colored lights which beckon you to come hither. On the other side of the path, you can see in the great distance large cities gleaming with opportunity for power and wealth; you probably will be tempted to stray off the path and investigate these deceptively bright and shiny people, and enticing things, but look down at the ground before you step. The ground is a blackish gray sticky clay. If you look closely, you will notice where others have stepped and sunken deep into this ooze.

If you take the time to consider your choices, a life of service to God is far more desirable and satisfying than a life of deceptive service to yourself. I say deceptive because you would not be serving yourself, but you would be serving the great deceiver, the evil one. In the end, you are left with nothing; you will be bankrupt. But I am getting ahead of myself.

Chapter 8

Dignity of Man

*La dignidad es un asunto que solo le importa
al ser humano*
— Livy, Ab Urbe Conditi (c. 29 B.C.)

*Dignity is a matter which concerns only
mankind*
— Livy, Ab Urbe Conditi (c. 29 B.C.)

When I look at the night sky and see the work of your
fingers—
the moon and the stars you set in place—
what are mere mortals that you should think about them,
human beings that you should care for them?
Yet you made them only a little lower than God
and crowned them with glory and honor.
You gave them charge of everything you made,
putting all things under their authority—
the flocks and the herds
and all the wild animals,
the birds in the sky, the fish in the sea,
and everything that swims the ocean currents.
(Bible, Psalms chapter 8, verses 4-8.)

I DO NOT UNDERSTAND EVERYTHING ABOUT OUR LIVES OR
the spirit realm, but I have learned enough to know that
Man is an extraordinary mix of the physical creation of this
world and the very breath of God. On the one hand, we
are made of the soil of the earth. Virtually every element

known to Man exists in the human body. Do you remember in Chemistry class learning the Periodic Table of Elements listed by their atomic weight? When I was in school, there were 102 elements, but I understand now there are 111, thanks to artificial construction. Physically we are like animals. We need to feed and drink. We mate, and we nest. Our nest may be larger than most other animals, but I have never seen an apartment complex more intricate or structurally sound than the honeycomb hives of bees. How many buildings do you know of which can be dropped three feet with virtually no damage and no casualties to the occupants? How are we different from animals? There is that opposable thumb. Some say that is the only thing that separates us from animals. Others say it is that we use tools, but it has been observed some animals use tools too. Maybe not Craftsmen tools, but they use twigs and the like. Some say it is our intelligence that separates us even though our brains or gray matter are very similar to that of some animals. Still, others say moral conscientiousness and self-determination separates us from animals. It is a clue in and of itself if we are seeking to separate ourselves from animals. These exclusive characteristics do not separate us from animals; they only differentiate. But we know that we *are* different and separate from animals. We intuitively know that we are a species unto ourselves. It is time to look at the other side of the coin.

I have already alluded to what makes Man unique, but I want to emphasize and expand the point. Man is biologically an animal; this has been established. What separates him from animals and therefore excludes him from being counted as an animal, is the following: Within Man resides the breath of God. I hope you do not write back and ask me to explain further because that is all I know about that. It is beyond my capacity to understand how the spiritual can coexist with the physical, but it does. Man is a creature with a physical body and a spirit, and this combination somehow precipitates the intellect and emotions. What is the breath of God? I can only define that by its activities. First, I have seen that this is what makes us an entirely new species. Second, this is what gives life to this old bag of bones. Third, and this is where things become less clear; the breath of God creates you as an individual with a free choice that will live beyond the shedding of your physical body. There are a lot of theories about these things, but I will refrain from venturing into what I call God's backyard. I will only share with you what He has shared with all of us in His word. It seems that once conceived, you become the proud owner of a spirit. In scripture, God said, "Before I formed you in the womb, I knew you." Also, humans are just slightly below the heavenly beings or angles. Our pedigree is quite prestigious. In effect, we are celestial creatures placed here to rule the world and to battle satan. Our role is not insignificant! "Man is God in a temporary state of self-forgetfulness."[1] That statement comes out of one of the Eastern-isms, but I forget which one; however, it did seem appropriate to mention here. I think Mankind has overlooked that while we are *not* gods, we *are* sons and daughters of The God entitled to all the honors, rights, and privileges thereto appertaining.

My purpose in writing these things is not to inflate your sense of self-love or ego, but to increase your love for others. I read a book by former Secretary of State Henry Kissinger[2]. What I walked away with is the idea of what is missing in our international relationships is the same thing that is missing in any dysfunctional interpersonal relationships; respect. That may be an oversimplification, but I do not believe so. You indeed are an exceptional and unique individual, placed here by God and given His spirit and talents to rule over this world, but the same is true of me! Having a high level of self-esteem is a good thing, but it is worthless if not coupled with a high level of the esteem of others. Every person on earth, no matter what station of life they may occupy, whether by effort or chance of birth, deserves the honoring of their inherent dignity, by the offering of respect. What right does one servant have to criticize another servant for shortcomings of their birth suit? What does this mean in practical terms? It signifies in all our interactions with fellow humans; we behave as if we were acting toward ourselves. It must always be at the forefront of our minds that others are worthy of honor and respect. Yes, my Sunshine, that means you must treat me like a King (I like the sound of that!) However, alas, I must treat you like a Queen (touché).

If you take this idea to its logical conclusion, the world would be a pretty nice place. Our motivation for this and any higher behavior is twofold; for personal satisfaction (or a good conscience), and compliance with our Father's wishes. The statement I made at the beginning of this section makes an important point. It is only when we wholly focus on our duty to humanity that we can forget ourselves and our inhibitions and assert who we are a coup sur (fr. for a certainty). When we are finally over ourselves, amazing things happen. We are free to express our God-inspired creativity and ingenuity. Think of the most beautiful music you can recall or the most awe-inspiring artwork you have experienced, and you will see one of two things. You will perceive a person's outward expression of their inward spirit, or you will view a person's outward expression of their inward frustration. Frustration is a failure to focus outside of themselves. If you are looking at yourself, you cannot see the beauty of God and the beauty of His creations.

You will only see your old bag of bones and play with them as you will; they will never satisfy you. I have experienced what some call art, and it is evident to anyone honest that is not art, at its best, it is narcissistic psychological masturbation (please forgive my coarseness). In the realm of intellectualism, this kind of work would quickly be discarded before anyone saw what a blunder we had made. Because we have a bit of God our Father within, we can think abstractly. In the history of Man, we have witnessed many specially gifted individuals who focused and shared their intellectual gifts with their fellow sojourners. We are the better for their generous contributions, and so too are those who our lives touch when we focus outward and allow our true selves to gift others. It is a vicious cycle; we should be so lucky to start such cycles to pass on from generation to generation!

When I was a student, I remember in one of my Psychology courses reading that various theories can explain all human behavior, except altruism. Psychology struggles to understand why a person would endanger him or herself or make a sacrifice for the well-being of a stranger when they will not gain any reward nor benefit from such action or behavior. I believe it is a characteristic of the spirit of God to react positively in a crisis intuitively. God created us to do good works. It is as natural for us to do good things because of the spirit of God in us, as it is for us to do bad things because of the weakness of our flesh. I wonder how the field of psychology would explain an individual doing something very evil just for the sake of being evil. I suspect it would be viewed as a mental disorder since it would not be purposeful behavior (just a note: no one wants to be a bad person; even gangbangers don't want their mama's to know what they do, right? Curious.). To be consistent, then one would have to say altruism is a mental disorder because, strictly speaking, it is not a purposeful behavior. Again, I am reminded of an Eastern religion's idea of Yin and Yang. We have opposing forces at work within us, and we are our own worst enemy on which the devil capitalizes.

I do not think we are responsible for everyone. Sometimes measured judgment is required when dealing with people. I will share with you a metaphor that may help you with your decision-making in these situations. This metaphor does not present a hard and fast rule, just a very general thought which may be useful. Imagine a graduated cylinder or a glass pitcher with evenly spaced markings on its side. The bottom inch of this container is our relationship with our Heavenly Father. If you are in good standing with God and you are meeting your responsibilities to Him, then you may pour your favorite color of water up to the first mark. The next inch of your device is your relationship with yourself.

Are you taking care of your own needs? I have already discussed that you need to meet your physical, emotional, intellectual, and spiritual needs before you can be effective in achieving your responsibilities to others. Much in the same manner as you cannot care for yourself until you have met the needs of your relationship with God. Are you beginning to see a pattern? If you have met your responsibilities to God and you have arranged the care of your self-relationship needs, then you may fill the container fuller to the next marking. You cannot advance to working on any other relationship until you have met the more important ones. How could you pour your pretty water and fill up a couple of sections and then skip some parts and return to filling? We must always dance to the rhythm of life. It is never right to do the wrong thing even if it is for a good reason. But I am getting ahead of myself.

Chapter 9

Rhythm of Life

*Ciertamente es de la experiencia de la belleza
y la felicidad, de la armonía ocasional entre
nuestra naturaleza y ambiente, donde sacamos
nuestro concepto de la vida divina.*
— George Santayana, <u>The Sense of Beauty</u>.
(1896).

*It is indeed from the experience of beauty
and happiness, from the occasional harmony
between our nature and environment, that we
draw our conception of the divine life.*
— George Santayana, <u>The Sense of Beauty</u>.
(1896).

To this point, I have spoken concerning very intimate
relationships in which we are to make every possible effort
to nurture in good health. The health of these relationships
determines the level of happiness, peace, joy, and contentment we experience in this life. It is my contention that
should we meet the needs and yes, the obligations which are
ours in these circumstances; we will be happy. The mysterious secret of life is, "If ye know these things, happy are
ye if ye do them." (Bible, John chapter 13, verse 17, King
James Version). I have nicknamed this cognitive and behav-
ioral concordance or the synchronization of our dance to the
rhythms of reality, which we already know. Life is smooth
and light as He said if we just let it happen. Mysterious life
is what goes on while you are making other plans. It goes on

right behind your back. I was practically already dead and buried while attending college. I had my life so well planned. However, not one bit of it ever materialized.

It would be so very nice if every human in the world had their glen in the woods with a white stone cottage overgrown with jasmine vines and a babbling brook just down the way. (I almost forgot. They would have lightning-fast Internet access too). There, they could live with the love of their life and make beautiful babies and live happily ever after. It would also be nice if McDonald's could make their Big Mac sandwich stand up straight instead of being all lopsided and spilling half the special sauce and lettuce inside the box, but somehow, I don't see that happening. Life in the real world involves having many kinds of relationships, with many types of people; sad as it is, they are as screwed up as you and I. How did God ever expect this thing called life would work? I suppose that may not be any of my business, at least not for the time being. Even the apostle Paul understood this when he encouraged the runaway slave named Onesimus to return to his owner. Paul knew that being a slave could not prevent one from living a happy and healthy life filled with peace and joy and contentment due to Christians having their residency in heaven with God not here on this physical earth.

God created this world, and he engineered all these various systems to work a certain way; if we conform to this rhythm of life, all is well. But, when Adam and Eve succumbed to the delusions of satan in the garden of Eden, evil was introduced into the world. This day was the darkest in human history. Evil ruined a perfectly good world. Now rocks in the soil frustrate farmers, and gardeners must contend with thorns on their beautiful flowers. Children must be careful not to play in the sun too long, and moms and dads spend a third of their lives providing for their families.

Humans are now susceptible to illness, and starvation is a reality. Without the influence of satan, the idea of crime and war would have been unimaginable.

The rhythms and systems are still in place, but sin in general gums up the works. What are we to do? If one is wise, he or she will learn of these so-called rhythms and systems and harmonize your life with them. Simply put, we need to use the components of life and the things of this world in the manner they were intended. This axiom applies to everything from our bodies to plants and our Father in heaven. For example, what is the intended purpose of our mind? Is it there to think? Thinking does accomplish a variety of tasks. We learn to avoid danger, and we learn to appreciate beauty. We learn to accommodate the needs and desires of our existence. However, there are things for which we do not use our brains. We do not use our brain like a hammer (that is unless you are a big-time wrestler), and we do not use our mind to hurt others. It is illogical to destroy your intellect for a few moments of pleasure, but it is logical to use your brain for non-harmful enjoyment. It is a good thing to use your brain to make this world a better place, and I believe God considers this good work. What is the use of the grain in the field? Is the use of grain for bread good? Is the use of grain to make L.S.D. or the drug commonly called acid good? Is making penicillin a good use of grain? I think it becomes clear everything in existence has the potential for use as intended, or for abuse. Wine, food, television, religion, sex, drugs, gambling, other people, sciences, politics, art, vitamin A… the list of things which can be used out of sync and thus abused, leading to addiction or slavery, or the voluntary loss of free will, is endless. None of it is suitable for anything.

When we walk through this life, we experience unavoidable contact and interaction with other people. Considering our knowledge of the rhythms of life set in motion by the

Creator, adherence to their principles ensures the enjoyment of this life, sometimes referred to as the human experiment. As stated earlier, this applies to everything. I know it is a rather bold statement, but I am willing to go out on a limb for that one, "For God has not given us a spirit of fear and timidity, but of power, love, and self-discipline." (Bible, 2nd Timothy chapter 1, verse 7). With this spirit, we can walk confidently through life, making decisions, and even some judgments. Not only can we, but we are *required* by life and God to do so. Some of life indeed happens to us, usually via others who are not cooperating with the systems of life, but it is even truer that *we* happen to our own life and the life of others. When we go about the business of living our lives, we have rules and responsibilities, and we have tools to help us with them. If you desire to harmonize your life energy with the life energy of this world, then you will need to utilize your tools for their intended purpose and meet your responsibilities, all within the confines of the rules. Now, does this sound mysterious and complex? It is not! Required for the successful ordering of one's life is to go with the flow. The "Tool" is your list of priorities and other resources like time and talent; the "Responsibilities" are the relationships in your life; the "Rules" for the use of tools in meeting your life responsibilities *are always* His words. I know all this may sound like "crazy-talk," but when the dust settles, you will see **the truth we already knew**.

There is more to life than what happens within your home. I hope you do not misunderstand. I estimate 75 % of the impact you are going to have on earth is within the confines of your home, and therefore, 75% of your energy should be naturally placed there. But that leaves 25% of your life resources unaccounted for, and we can't have that! John Donne so eloquently said some 400 years ago (1624) in his Devotions, "No man is an island, entire of itself; every man is a piece of the continent." There is our vocation, education, religious rituals, social and political obligations to consider. With our limited economy, having only 25% of our life resources available, necessity requires shrewd time management and understanding limitations.

We are not speaking of money here; we are talking about the most valuable currency called time, and our daily allowance of energy or ability. We call it earning a living, but what it boils down to is this; we give away a piece of our life, and with a paycheck, a piece of our life is redeemed. Our "life," our "time" is our most precious commodity. Where we spend our "lifetime" determines what we will get out of it. If we are spending our "lifetime" on material things, then material things are what we get. If we spend our "lifetime" on the ethereal, then we will reap spiritual things. Do you see that our "lifetime" is our currency while here on earth? There is no such thing as "quality time," that was just a marketing blurb sent out by satan trying to confuse things. We cannot modify time in any particular way and make it more valuable. The best we can do is spend our time wisely.

In the same manner, we are responsible for the meeting of relational needs with our Creator and our self and our spouse and children; we also have responsibilities to fellow sojourners on this adventure. God's word says, "Share each other's burdens, and in this way obey the law of Christ." (Bible, Galatians chapter 6, verse 2) and "for we are each responsible for our conduct." (Bible, Galatians chapter 6, verse 5). I know you will hear someone say the Bible contradicts itself. I concede, it seems that way at times, but you will find this is not true. The limited capacity of language produces these pseudo clashes. These situations are particularly fertile ground for many delusions. There seems to be a proclivity among society to choose one or the other statement as truth instead of dissimilating the true meaning of both reports. It does not take a great deal of effort to harmonize the above ideas if you trust God gave us these two thoughts for our betterment. I try to avoid making very many big statements, but one I am willing to make is this one. You can always trust the words of God! If there seems to be a problem with His words, relax, it is all in your head. His Word is perfect. It is us who get a little off-center sometimes but be patient, and He will realign you soon.

I think the above conundrum refers to our duty to go about doing good works in helping others (this implies you too will be helped.) Nevertheless, the responsibility and accountability for your life squarely rest on your shoulders. Remember, "The soul who sins is the one who will die." (Bible, Ezekiel chapter 18, verse 20.) The person who sins is the one who will die. The child is not punished for the parent's sins, and the parent is not punished for the child's sins. Righteous people are rewarded for their moral behavior, and wicked people are punished for their wickedness. However, the effects of one's sins do lie at the feet of the innocent.

If we were to live detached entirely from the world, we would not be able to fulfill the purpose for which God has created us. If humankind is designed to do good works, and helping our brother carry his load is one of these good works, then of necessity, we must interact with the world outside our intimate family of origin and family of procreation. For me, this is where life becomes risky. I remember as a young man riding the elevator to the top of the Transamerica building in San Francisco; looking out over the entire city, contemplating just how many different lives there are out there, and thinking that each person must feel just like I do; that only their experience is real, and others' lives are just background noise. But that is not right. We are all connected. It is like the Honey mushrooms they found in Northeastern,

Oregon. It seemed there were hundreds of thousands of these mushrooms, but it was, in fact, one single organism, one giant plant covering 10 square kilometers or 2,384 acres of forestland (imagine 1,665 football fields). We are all connected and made of the same stuff. When we hurt another, we injure our self, and when we help another, we help ourselves. That sounds sweet and nice, but it is not just a fluffy thought; it is what we learn from the Bible, and it is literal.

Jesus said, "…And the King will say, 'I tell you the truth when you did it to one of the least of these my brothers and sisters, you were doing it to me!'." He further said, "'I tell you the truth when you refused to help the least of these, my brothers and sisters, you were refusing to help me." whatever you did not do for one of the least of these, you did not do for me." (Bible, Matthew, chapter 25, verses 40 and 45). The question we need to answer is, how do we meet our obligations to those outside the cocoon of our families without being injured or neglecting ourselves? I hope you like to surf because this is one of those slippery slope situations.

In this world, *we walk alone together*. Remember the colored water analogy and that the first mark is to tend to our relationship with our heavenly Father. Next, we are to care for ourselves by providing for all our needs and meeting all our responsibilities. Then we are to fulfill our relationship promises to our spouse and then our children. I believe that brings us to the fifth mark on the container labeled extended family or the family of your origin. That's right, darling; you have a responsibility to me. However, I fall at number five on the list of priorities, but still, I changed your diapers, and now it's your turn to change mine. Yuck! What an awful metaphor. Sadly, it is the case for some, and I fervently hope not for us. (There's that pride again!)

The point is into our lives come voluminous opportunities to perform good works, but we are not expected or even capable of responding in the positive to each one. We must be wise or, as Jesus said, "...Look, I am sending you out as sheep among wolves. So be as shrewd as snakes and harmless as doves." (Bible, Matthew, chapter 10, verse 16.) Now how do we do that? A giant boulder in my path prevented me from learning when to limit my efforts. However, as is usual in these circumstances, the big rock in the road was me, and the wisdom, which eluded me, was plainly before me. I just had to settle down and quit stirring up dust in my inpatient wanderings for the answer to become apparent. Now I am embarrassed in front of myself and God at how obvious the solution is. "For God has not given us a spirit of fear and timidity, but of power, love, and self-discipline." (Bible, 2nd Timothy chapter 1, verse 7).

With this spirit, we can walk confidently through life making decisions and even some judgments, remember? Today I told my niece she could not move in with me. Making that decision surprised me. She is in foster care, which is good but still less then desirable, and I thought I was going to take her in; I suddenly realized both my house and my life are full and bulging just a bit. I was surprised at myself because, supposedly, I am all about being the "good guy," and there was an opportunity to do a good and significant thing, and I declined. I do not feel guilty about it, but I do feel disappointed. I know I could have made a positive impact on her life as I did for her brothers.

I wish I had more resources, like time and money. It occurred to me; sometimes, just having talent is not enough to help someone. You sometimes do need resources or access to other people's skills and resources before you can activate your own. You see, we are all connected, and we need each other; I think that is what extended family, friends, and fellow Christians are all about. The synergistic effect of working together allows us to do wonderfully amazing things. If I knew of someone with an extra room or someone with a larger home that I could use, I would have been able to accept her. (Synergism- the combination of effects being greater than their sum. exempli gratia. Two plus two equals nine.)

Never be afraid to do the right thing no matter what the apparent cost because our Father is wealthy, and the deceiver is always trying to pad the cost, but God can see past his bluff. It is never right to do the wrong thing for the right reason. It is a bluff of the great deceiver. God is good, and he cares for his own always. You can take that to the bank! Just because an opportunity to do a good thing presents itself does not make you an indentured servant to do so. For an opportunity to become a responsibility, several variables must be present. First, of course, there needs to be a deficient situation. Secondly, you must possess the necessary tools for the task. These include the time and talent and access to other resources required. The most useful tool in these circumstances is the self-care tool of priority. You must always take care of your higher responsibilities before you begin to tend to others. It is never right to leave undone higher priorities to tend to lower ones. Remember, your God is also the God of everyone else, and if he takes care of you, then he will take care of them. A faithful follower of our heavenly Father is to concern him/herself with the business of honoring God, doing good works toward others, and subduing the earth but not to the degree of abusing the tools or talents He has given. That would be a slothful service. Like my grandpa, Eddie said, "Take good care of your tools, and they will take good care of you." I am a little bit proud of my tools, even if they are old-fashioned. My Father gave me a body and a mind and a spirit. He made certain adjustments on my body and mind to bump up the performance a bit, but he does that with all His special creations. I hope I don't tear it up too much while using it here on this earth and in this life. I am glad I got full coverage to cover any damage I may do. He offered it to me, and I said, "Sure, I need all the help I can get." I appreciate his generosity, and I will do my best not to wreck it! But I am getting ahead of myself.

Chapter 10

Forgiveness

*La alegría incomprensible de perdonar y de ser
perdonado crea una éxtasis que despierta la
envidia de los dioses.*
— Elbert Hubbard, <u>The Note Book.</u> (1927).

*"The ineffable joy of forgiving and being
forgiven forms an ecstasy that might well
arouse the envy of the gods.*
— Elbert Hubbard, <u>The Note Book.</u> (1927).

IT IS A FACT OF LIFE THAT SHOULD YOU VENTURE OUTSIDE
your fortress of solitude; you will be injured. You cannot
walk in the rain and avoid being struck by a raindrop. Our
life here on this blue planet is like a giant pinball game. Do
I not sound like a wise old man now? The "icky one" puts
a bad vibe out into this physical realm in the form of a steel
ball, it slams into this guy, and he takes it and fires it across
the way at his wife. She is not going to have a good day.
After dropping little Billy-Bob at pre-school and on her way
to work, a driver in front of her suddenly slammed on the
brakes, causing her coffee to spill on her dress. She immediately reached for that steel ball, which beaned her earlier
and flings it straight up the driver's tailpipe! He went on his
way and delivered his donuts right upstairs to my office. I
owed him $4.40, and all I had was a twenty. I asked him if
he would go downstairs and get change, and POW out of
nowhere came out that steel ball right at my ear! He went
downstairs and got change, and we concluded our business.

I took that devilish steel ball and put it in my coat pocket. Later that night, when I was talking with my heavenly Father, I buried it in the backyard. Oh, sure I could have thrown that steel ball at Grandma when she called that afternoon and complained that I don't visit often enough, but the way I figure it that little influence from the darkness had caused enough trouble for one day, and I just wanted it to end here and now with me. If more people would take that stupid little steel ball and put it in their coat pocket, there would be a lot less rage in the world. It seems to be human nature to keep passing around those things.

I trust you have been around long enough to realize it is not necessary to step outside our intimate sphere of existence to have our dignity breached. Sadly, it appears those who are most dear to us are also most prone to betray us. A relationship is an implied contractual partnership based on mutual trust, knowledge, time, respect, acceptance, and commitment. Its very nature is a vulnerability. Refer to your graduated cylinder of prioritized relationships. All relationships consist of the same components I just mentioned. However, they differ in intensity and significance. A healthy lifestyle is using all our many parts of existence for their intended purpose and appropriating our life energy among our many relationships. The lower the relationship on the graduated cylinder, the more life energy required to meet its responsibilities appropriately. The payoff for synchronization with the flow of this world is HAPPINESS! Not the wild party down kind of happiness (there are moments of this from time to time) but more of the peace and joy type of happiness. The resultant life is one of calm contentment even in the eye of the storm. "And you will know the truth, and the truth will set you free" (Bible, John chapter 8, verse 32).

It happened to me when I was ten years old. It probably happened earlier, but this one incident when I was 10 is the earliest significant recollection I have of when it happened. I met the world, the world met me, and it did not like me much. I was a fifth-grade student at Temperance Kutner elementary school in Fresno, California. I towered over my classmates, and it appeared I was destined to be an above-average size man like my father; however, I was very meek in spirit. I admired Larry Mendoza, who was shorter than average in stature, but his easy smile and confident and dignified demeanor naturally installed him as leader of the schoolyard. I am unclear why, but it seemed to have something to do with my size that one day at the bus stop around the corner of my house, I found myself an unwitting opponent in a fight with Larry. I had no desire to fight with him; I had no quarrel with him.

I held a secret admiration for this little giant. As more and more kids gathered around, the encouraging roar of the crowd grew louder and louder; I noticed Larry kept glancing at the group first to the left then to the right. It was as if he was confirming this is what they wanted. I told Larry I wouldn't fight him because I had no reason. However, he would not lower his fist. I pleaded with him and said to him that I did not want to hurt him, and I refused to fight him. Then something came over me like a dark black storm cloud, and my spirit ached. Why would someone who I held in such high regard want to cause me pain? I began to cry and continued to plead; I did not want to fight, and I did not want to hurt him. The taunts of the surrounding kids became louder, and I began to sob, and then Larry threw his tightened fist into my face, and I bled. My nose is still crooked. It is evil in this world, and it attacks us every day. Strangest thing, though, it almost always uses those who we love to deliver the blow.

Not all attacks are as overt as the story I shared with you. At your place of work, there is the supervisor you have developed a friendship only to have you overlooked for a pro-motion because they are envious of your talents and skills. It is also common for individuals to have spouses withhold emotional intimacy because of fears learned in childhood. Even your brothers and sisters in the Spirit sometimes will view you with suspicion when you enthusiastically support good work. Without considering the diseases that plague us or other hazards of living that our frail bodies are subject to, evil impacts us every day. Whatever we can do to minimize its effect is worth our earnest consideration. One of these ethereal tools is forgiveness. At first mention, it appears that the activity of mercy is something which would be of ben-efit to perpetrators against us; however, this is not the case. Have you ever noticed that the scriptures address the reader directly? In English composition, this refers to the voice of the writer. Voice considers first, second, or third person and past, present, or future tense. Other considerations include perspectives, audience, and cases, and so on. I do not con-sider myself an expert, but I have studied a couple of foreign languages, and that opened my eyes to understand English a little better. I will continue to make my point. In scripture, even when the subject of other people arises, it is interest-ing to note that the information being communicated deals not with the other individual, but instead, it deals with our interaction with them. God's word is concerned with me as the reader, and when the topic of forgiveness presents itself, it is from my point of view and for my benefit. Forgiveness, as discussed in the Bible, is an act of self-care.

How do you forgive someone who has done you wrong? Maybe, you need to check yourself before overlooking an offense. Look at yourself; you are the total of your parent's little adventure. Now you are all grown up, you think none of that matters anymore, but it does, and it does in a big way! You are the result of your mom's genes and your dad's genes.

Add to that a splash of childhood trauma(s), and a pinch of unique individuality, just a smidgen of environmental culture, and le viola' there you are! So, you are holding someone's soul over the fire deciding whether to forgive. Sister, the decision to forgive or not forgive is a no-brainer.

Forgiving someone who has violated you is like rebooting a home alarm system. It is both necessary and in your best interest. When an individual violates a relationship with you, they have taken something that was not theirs, and that hurts. The loot taken was your dignity. When you forgive the culprit, you reacquire that lost property. But if the other person is the perpetrator, why do you do the personal inventory? First, personal inventories are always beneficial. In this case, a tool that affords you a clear perspective. Any time we can see things as they are, it is to our advantage. In a situation when a person has committed an offense against you, even though you are a victim, you are in a position of power, and with power comes responsibility. You have free will; you have the choice to condemn the guilty individual in your heart. It is also true that you are in control of your thoughts and actions; you are in control of your world (your interior life). Truth allows them to have peace and joy in this world of chaos. I recall a note found on the wall of a Nazi concentration camp, "I believe in the sun when it is not shining. I believe in love, even when I feel it not. I believe in God even when He is silent." Jesus said, "For my yoke is easy to bear, and the burden I give you is light" (Bible, Matthew chapter 11, verse 30). He also said, "If you forgive those who sin against you, your heavenly Father will forgive you." (Bible, Matthew chapter 6, verse 14). At this point, daughter, you may be asking yourself, "Where is he going with this?" I am trying to show you the big picture that is in the small event of forgiving someone who has sinned against you. In this physical life, we are living things that are not as they appear.

Reality resides in the spiritual realm, and it consists of ethereal things. I hope you can see that forgiving someone is not something you do for the other person, but you do for Jesus and yourself. Sadly, in most cases, it does very little for the offender, even though there is a tremendous opportunity for learning in this circumstance.

There is an effect I call a reverse curve. The more you forgive others, the more you can forgive yourself, and most importantly, the more you will be able to accept the forgiveness we have in the Christ. satan's most successful delusions are convincing forgiven people that they may not possess forgiveness and convincing un-forgiven people that they do not deserve forgiveness. I would think that his second most successful delusion is convincing some that they do not require forgiveness. Getting back to how to forgive, I would like to expand my discussion of checking yourself. It is so easy to see other people's crap, but to be fair, we must consider our crap. I think the apostle Paul offered sound advice when he suggested that when we find one of our brothers in a sinful situation that we, "Should restore him gently. But watch yourself, or you also may be tempted." Tempted to do what? We may be tempted to think more highly of ourselves than we ought. We may be tempted to be overly harsh. Who are we to condemn anyone? If we are honest, it is only by the grace of God that we have not gone to the same sinful situation. Forgiving people who have hurt you helps you heal and feels good. The commandments of God are really for our good and not His. But I am getting ahead of myself.

Chapter 11

Depression

En cada vida un poco de lluvia tiene que caer. Algunos días tienen que estar oscuros y deprimidos.
— Henry Wadsworth Longfellow,
"The Rainy Day" (1842).

Into each life, some rain must fall. Some days must be dark and dreary.
—Henry Wadsworth Longfellow,
"The Rainy Day" (1842).

I HESITATE TO CONTINUE WRITING ABOUT THIS NEXT TOPIC not because I question your intellectual prowess but because it's so very depressing. You are familiar with the knowledge that I am susceptible to periods of melancholy, and I am concerned that one day, you may become beset yourself as it seems to run in the family. This fact has urged me to alertness whenever I heard the subject addressed, whether in casual conversation or more formally in the written word. Further, I have been motivated to spend more than a little time pondering the mystery that is depression.

When sin entered the world, everything was tainted. The thistles began to grow, and rocks appeared in the soil. I believe this was when we turned from vegetarians to omnivores (meat and veggies.) Our bodies weakened and made us more prone to accidents and illnesses. I also think that our minds were diminished to some degree, thus, leading to mental limitations, inconvenient handicaps, and disease.

Depression is a big old ugly black hole that sucks the life out of whatever or whomever it can find. It is a black cloud, or maybe a deep dark cave. It is different things for different people, but whatever form it takes, it is bad news. I have wrestled with this beast and fought with all my might; I have snuggled up with it and enjoyed a nice three-month nap. I hate it, and I need it. It reminds me of what is important and keeps me on track. There is nothing better than putting on a hot pot of coffee and curling up with a good depression. Do not be deceived; it is seductive. One day I hope to understand it better.

When I consider what depression is, I can't help feeling that what many people refer to as depression may involve several varieties. Perhaps our language lacks the diversity to discriminate among this group of similar ailments. For example, is the depression one experiences at their high school's 25th reunion the same as the depression experienced at the loss of your home to fire? Is the depression of menopause the same as that of prolonged envy? There must be a half dozen different kinds of depression, and if that is a true statement, then shouldn't there be at least that many methods of treatment or at the very least a variety of means for coping? Darling, do you now see why I was hesitant about going down this path? *"It's* creepy, and *it's* kooky, mysterious and spooky, and it's altogether ooky..."[1] Where do we go from here? Again, the beginning seems to be a good starting point. When Adam and Eve first sinned and brought evil into this world. Thus, the beginning of all depression. The ground brings forth rocks and weeds to the farmer, and the dust of the earth brings forth ailments and depression to humanity. Is it not weird that when I am attempting to understand grief, the subject of sin pops right up? Humans are hard-wired for depression, just as we are hard-wired for spiritual awareness. The rhythm of life strikes again!

I recall as a young teenager thinking when I finally get my driver's license; everything will be great. My life will be complete, and only happy days lie before me. "My future's so bright I gotta wear shades,"[2] as the song goes. I must have been a real cocky teen because I remember waiting until the day after my 16th birthday to get my license to prove to my mother I had self-control. I do not remember the circumstances, but I do remember she and I both being angry and secretly sad. I suspect that may have been one of those moments of parent-child separation, which so frequently occurs during adolescence. It is to my dismay and utter disappointment I now report my expectations were not correct. I am confident I was anti-correct. You see, sweet child, my life has been downhill ever since acquiring the sacred driver's license. Perhaps I am overstating the case but, suffice it to say where I anticipated loosening cares and responsibilities at the acquisition of said driver's license was in truth the point at which I seemingly began to hoard additional cares, concerns, and responsibilities. To be sure if possessing worries is an asset, then I am indeed a very wealthy man. "Do not cry for me, Argentina…"[3] or Brazil or Chile or any other South American country, I only wish my country, my precious *la Tierra Linda,* to cry for me. We must be brave and proceed onward to the subject at hand.

Once again, it is wise to address the three realms of existence and both internal and external influences when discussing the human-animal (oxymoron.) When I think about a person becoming depressed, I envision an individual who has the usual symptoms such as sadness, lack of energy, inability to concentrate, dissatisfaction with current circumstances, and a sense that things are going to be like this forever. Clinically speaking, these conditions must remain persistent for two weeks to be considered a significant depression and not merely a case of the blues, which may not be the precise clinical jargon. If you ever fall into this way, I hope you will reach out for help. Medical science has observed when a person becomes depressed; there seems to be a slowdown in the brain's activity level. Researchers by the agency of diligent study discovered nerves in the central nervous system, which appear responsible for one's mood. It is noted that depressed individuals exhibit a significantly less amount of neural activity than those of a non-depressed individual. Therefore, they correctly postulated that manipulating the dendrites would effect a positive change in an individual's mood. However, does manipulating the body's chemistry address the issue of depression? If I happen upon a man who is suicidal, will the manipulation of his brain chemistry change his intentions? Is it that simple? If a depressed person is given chemical manipulation via a pill, is it reasonable to expect that he or she will experience a return to the normal functioning, and with this restorative manipulation, will we observe the expression of relief from even the most disagreeable moods? Will their countenance improve, and vigor is restored? Will this person regain the ability to concentrate, and will he or she feel that life is worth living, with endless possibilities?

In some cases, the answer will be yes. More correctly, some people are depressed because of a malfunction in their neuron department, but it also could be a glitch in the endocrine system. There are glands in our bodies that produce hormones (more than 50 varieties) and the messages these hormones send or do not send. It seems to have a great deal to do with one's mood. In the same manner as with neurotransmitters, so are hormones. The nervous system has its sympathetic and parasympathetic homeostasis action as the endocrine system has its endocrine and exocrine sources producing a stable balance. It is a Yin-Yang thing; if there is an interruption in normal functioning, clinical depression occurs. Once again, chemical manipulation would seem to be an appropriate remedy.

"Our whole life was in that house, all our family photos and the kids baby things, it is all gone now!" Can you even imagine how it would feel to lose everything if your home burned down? I think I would have a real sensation of pain deep in my chest. I imagine I may experience actual physical pain. I certainly understand such a significant loss could cause one to become depressed. I am sad to say I could recite scores of scenarios involving a loss of some kind that could elicit a depressive reaction. I am unsure this is the same depression as described above. This current circumstance consists of an event outside the body evoking a depression. If I may add for your consideration, an individual subjected to attack or abuse of their mind/body can incur a depressive state, would that further complicate the matter at hand? Also, if you recall at the beginning of this section, I briefly alluded to a prolonged emotional state of envy, bringing about depression. Are you overwhelmed yet? I do not have all the answers, but I do see some clues, and I want to share them with you; they have helped me, and they may help you.

The question I have, is everything we call depression really depression? Is depression one destination, and all the above scenarios only various arrival patterns? Or, are there multiple destinations that all happen to be depressing? Popular opinion is that major clinical depression is a central nervous system dysfunction. More specifically, it is a deficiency of neurotransmitters within the brain. It has been postulated this deficiency can be an inherited genetic trait or an effect of acute or chronic trauma. Further, this trauma can be either physical or emotional or a combination.

Some people inherit a mental illness called bipolar affective disorder or manic-depressive disorder. These people have a variety of cycles of hyperactivity and then depression.

Another related mental illness is Depressive disorder. There are several variations of this disorder with varying durations and intensities. Depressions precipitated by acute physical trauma can be due to a biological illness or a bodily injury or physical shock. Depressions caused by chronic physical trauma can be due to persistent organic illness or physical injuries, enduring effects. Emotional trauma is a frequent source of unhappiness, whether a one-time event or an ongoing stressful circumstance. Finally, depression can be a semi self-inflicted ailment via stinking thinking. This flavor receives the "semi self-inflicted" prefix because the patient learns negative thought patterns from his or her environment.

It seems depression is a reduction in neural electrical activity, and the symptoms associated are presently the retarding of physical, mental, and emotional functioning at clinically significant intensities and durations. What I find to be the most intriguing thing about depression, however, is the etiology of this condition. What causes depression? Genetic inheritance, physical illness, physical injury, physical shock, emotional abuse, emotional loss, material loss, low self-esteem, envy, hyper-vigilance, and violation of conscience. What is the point? I know some causes of depression and what it does to my body and how it affects my mood. Where the rubber meets the road is: does knowing these things help me to understand how to cope with depression or hope beyond all hope, does it suggest a correction? The most common treatments seem to be chemical manipulation. The next would be psychological and sociological psychotherapies derived from a dozen or so various philosophies. These approaches have had their successes, but there has yet to emerge a successful and appropriate treatment for depression.

If you will indulge me one more time, permit me to review this whole depression thing. Your body can depress you, and your negative thinking can depress you. Other people's disrespectful behavior and emotional interaction can depress you. The loss of physical possessions and intimate relationships can depress you as can even the threat of insecurity. I do not know if all depression is the same thing, but it does seem our bodies and our moods express themselves in the same manner in response to these depressing scenarios. At this point, I would like to share the answers to depression, which has afforded me some relief.

If I find myself at the bottom of the deep dark cave of depression, the first thing I realize is I must get myself to the doctor or psychiatrist for some antidepressants and possibly some anti-anxiety medication. I know this is not the most pleasant thought. Still, God gave us intelligence, and I believe part of "subduing the earth" command (Bible, Genesis chapter 1, verse 28) involves the pursuit of all kinds of knowledge and utilizing it for our betterment. The best chemical remedies for depression have yet to be discovered, the ones we have so far are of some use. The same is true of psychotherapy. I think there are grains of truth in most of these philosophical theories, and it may be beneficial to talk with someone trained in their practice. I believe a person familiar with God's word is most qualified if they are mature. Also, group therapy is most useful for depressed persons, as misery loves company. No, I am kidding. However, there is something very helpful in learning you are not the only one in the world with these crazy thoughts.

Along with this line of thought, I would like to share; I think most types of depression are deceptive delusions of satan, which brings us to my next suggestion of meditation. During my bouts with depression, I found a sort of regrouping or re-evaluation of my current circumstances to be one of the most efficient tools. I am embarrassed to admit it, but I sometimes forget what real life is. The worries and unimportant desires overtake me. If I take the time to pray and ask my Father to show me where I am in life and what he wants me to be busy doing. It clears things up. The biggest surprise to me is it is not complicated. All I must do is love Him and love and care for my "real" needs and love and care for my loved ones. It is utterly amazing to me that all God wants from me is to love him, and He says to serve Him all I must do is do good works for His children, and He will count that as doing good things for Him! Also, I take my heavenly vitamins daily. Sacred vitamins are thoughts of heaven. Taking these Heavenly vitamins is a pleasant chore.

The next thing I recommend is engaging in an activity that accomplishes something. I suggest a simple task to begin with as depressed people have very little energy. Achievement is a potent elixir, even in small doses. However, one of the most potent prescriptions for depression is to do something for another person. There are two variables to consider when dosing this cure, first it is the deed itself. The act can range in strength from one, which is a "thoughtful gesture" to a "fulfilling a need." The second variable to consider is choosing a recipient. This individual could be a loved one or a stranger. The further removed from the recipient, the more pronounced the effect. Therefore, for full strength and maximum effectiveness, one would choose the two most extreme variables to "meet a need" of a "stranger."

The truth is so simple, and it is standing right there amid the words of the Bible to study. The Bible is a gift to us from God and Jesus and the Holy Spirit. Life is good. God is good! But I am getting ahead of myself.

PERSONAL

Chapter 12

Relationship with God

Mas cerca esta el que el respirar, y más cerca
que las manos y los pies.
— Lord Tennyson,
The Higher Pantheism (1869).

Closer is he than breathing, and nearer than
hands and feet.
— Lord Tennyson,
The Higher Pantheism (1869).

MY SWEET, SWEET TERA LINDA, I HAD NO IDEA I HAD THESE many words in me. I want so much to share with you everything I have learned so you can live the life I dream for you. I want you to discover the talent given to you by the Creator and to use these in a way that brings you joy, brings to others happiness and brings honor to your Heavenly Father. It is my hope for you that you will find a husband who supports and facilitates you if this is your desire. Also, it would not disappoint me if you brought grandchildren into this world. It is my wish your positive life experiences outweigh your negative life experiences. May your yoke be easy, and your burden light as He has promised. May you find and hold on to peace and joy forever. May you always be a bright light to the entire world as you always have been in my house. I love you.

I have shown you God was the Creator of the Cosmos and the Earth and everything in it, especially Man and Woman. I have shown you the Holy Bible is the very words of God, and His Son came to this planet and prepared a means of atonement for our violations of the Law of Sin and Death. He also made a method of communication between Him and us, and He offers us Communion. Our Father has given us His wisdom to assist us in living a life saturated with peace and joy. Finally, He has given us a family here on this Blue Ball for fellowship, education, worship, communion, work, and the ministration of care. "Surely goodness and mercy will follow me all the days of my life..." (Bible, Psalms 23.)

During my lifetime, I have heard it said many times you could do anything you desire if you put your mind to it. That statement is incorrect, and I think it is responsible for a lot of heartaches. Further, it has created despondency, especially among the young people of the previous few generations. Not all who desire a career in professional sports or desire to become famous actors or musicians will attain their goal. Only a handful may become the President of the United States, and realistically how many people have what it takes to be a doctor, teacher, or astronaut? (I will discuss this in greater detail later.) These thoughts brought me to a question. Why were we created? This question precipitates another. What are we to do while we are here?

I do not want to alarm you, Darling, but there was a time after your mother left our family I wanted to die. That is not precise in meaning. I yearned to end my life. I am not particularly proud of this fact, but I am not particularly ashamed of it either. I often cite if it had not been for my children, I might very well not be alive today. You may ask yourself what does that mean and what does this have to do with our current discussion? I will answer those two questions. During the darkest, coldest, and most alone time in my life, I made a brilliant discovery that saved me. Not only did it rescue me, but it has also helped to clarify and define my life. I owe my sense of satisfaction with life to this sole discovery. Drum roll, please! I discovered the meaning of life is in a single word: Love. Think about it for a minute. All the stuff we call life is relationships. Humanity's purpose is to have a love relationship with God, to have a love relationship with itself, and to have a love relationship with others. There is tremendous wealth in these words. There is spectacular wealth in this one word. There is great wealth in Love. The greatest wealth is Love.

Now I have zeroed in on the heart of the matter, let me back out a bit. What saved me was what I had learned in an object lesson taught to me by you and your brothers. While love is at the center of it all, it is a relationship that became a lifeline for me. More precisely, it was a relationship with God and a relationship with me, which saved me, and it is what I learned from my children. My love for you, the boys, and my love for God would not allow me to end myself. Thank you.

God created us for his pleasure. This statement may appear a demeaning state of being; however, this would be a false conclusion encouraged by the father of lies. To be created by God and in his image, no less is a high honor. The only thing the Creator of everything commands of us is to love him. Without choice, there is no love. There is one more thing I would like to say about this, which puzzles me. He allows us to say no. I don't get it, but he leaves himself wide open to rejection. We mere humans are not without power even in the spiritual realms. We can hurt God.

There are many kinds of relationships to be had in this life, but all relationships share several essential characteristics. Sweetheart if you wish to answer the call that resides in all of humanity for a connection to the source; if you want to have a relationship with our Heavenly Father; if you're going to obey the Creator's command to love Him; then you need to treat this relationship like you would any other relationship, however, this relationship needs to be at the top of all the priority lists of your life (after all, he is the tallest). All relationships require several vital components if they are to thrive. Because one of the most basic of human rights even in the presence of God Almighty, is to say no, all relationships must begin with the choice of yes. At the onset, the individual must desire to decide between pursuing a relationship. Next, there is the dedication of time. Time is one of human's most precious commodities and an indispensable ingredient in the soup of relationships. By spending your time wisely, you will gain knowledge about the object of your relationship, and this knowledge may develop affection for the other participant in this dish. Eventually, the time will come requiring more choice and decision. Do you accept the object of your love as they stand before you without any modification? If you agree, then do you commit yourself to the relationship and all its implied maintenance responsibilities? If so, the soup is done and let the celebration feast begin! All relationships should be marked by celebrations, don't you think?

During my studies of the relationship our Creator desires to have with us, I discovered that from my perspective, it is pretty much one-sided. What he craves from us does not compare to what he wants to give us. He wants us to love Him, spend some time talking with Him, and he would appreciate it if we would thank Him for what he does for and gives to us. Previously, I shared with you these facts: He gave us His Holy Bible for knowledge about this life and the next life. He sent His son Jesus to settle our sin account. He established the Church, so we would have a spiritual family for support, which we sorely need in these difficult times. There are many other things he has done for us, and he has given to us. Are you breathing right now? Thank God for the air.

In the very beginning, God was quite clear about what direction Man was to take on this mortal coil. In Genesis,

Adam and Eve are instructed to rule the Earth and the animals. That seems straightforward. They are also told to be fruitful. This Admonition interests me because my studies in psychology revealed a base need of Man is to attain a sense of accomplishment. Next in Genesis is the direction to increase in number and fill the Earth. I think Man has taken this to heart, as there are more than 7 billion of us filling this sphere. However, considering His next two directions, maybe we still have a bit more work to do. It stated we were to subdue the Earth and gain control of it.

I do not deny humanity has made notable progress in the subduing and controlling of the Earth, but there is much more room for expanding the realm of our control. We have partially harnessed the nuclear power of the element plutonium, but we still cannot seem to be able to tame the winds of a tornado or hurricane. We will harness these powers someday. Someday we will be not only able to predict earthquakes, but we will be able to prevent them. Sometime very soon, we will settle on the Arctic and Antarctic poles as well as the ocean floors and the surface of the Moon. I know this may sound like a wild fantasy, but as we used to say around the house when you kids were young, "it could happen!" There is one more thing about these directions we find in Genesis. These framed words are within the commission to take care of the charge. We are to manage the Earth well, not just exploit its resources. You may think I am a bit on the weird side, but these directions excite me. God is anxious to see how far we can go in fulfilling his prescriptions. We have already come so far, especially in the past 100 years. Think of all the medical breakthroughs and the practical value of the industrial revolution. Here in America, look at what we have accomplished in the agricultural and computer sciences. The full impact of the World Wide Web will not be felt for many years. There have been more technological advances in the previous century than there were in the proceeding 5,900 years. If you ponder what the future will bring, it is so exciting that it is almost frightening.

He offers direction in life, he instructs how to live life, and he provides His assistance in living life. Always be true to yourself. But I am getting ahead of myself.

Chapter 13

Relationship with Self

Es difícil exigir que un hombre este miserable
mientras él se sienta digno de sí mismo y
declara ser parte de la familia del gran Dios
que lo ha hecho.
— Abraham Lincoln, discurso, Washington,
D.C., (14 de septiembre, 1862).

"It is difficult to make a man miserable while
he feels worthy of himself and claims kindred
to the great God who made him.
— Abraham Lincoln, speech, Washington,
D.C., (Sept. 14, 1862).

NO MATTER HOW ADVANCED WE BECOME, WE WILL STILL
have our basic needs. God promises to provide us with food,
clothing, and shelter, so we never have to worry about those
things if we are faithful to him and his commandments. I
must confess when I wrote that last line, I recoiled a bit. The
thought of obeying commands does not seem pleasant. Jesus
said, "For my yoke is easy to bear, and the burden I give you
is light." (Bible, Matthew chapter 11, verse 30), so I thought
it would be a good idea to look at what He requires of us.
There is this fantastic verse in one of the Gospels where Jesus
answers the question,

> "Which is the greatest commandment in the Law?"
> Jesus replied, "You must love the LORD your God
> with all your heart, all your soul, and all your mind.

This is the first and greatest commandment. A second is equally important: 'Love your neighbor as yourself.' The entire law and all the demands of the prophets are based on these two commandments."

(Bible, Matthew, chapter 22, verses 37-40)

In this one statement, the meaning of life is simply and beautifully laid out. I found in these words a frame on which to hang my philosophy of life. For a simple man like your father, I need a simple formula to arrange the priorities of my life and a reference to look to when life presents difficult situations. On my list of priorities, my relationship responsibilities to God come first always. Next, on my list, are my responsibilities to myself. Self-care is not stated overtly in Jesus' reply; however, it is implied. How can we "…Love your neighbor as yourself" (Bible, Matthew, chapter 22, verse 39), if we don't love ourselves? Therefore, the second entry on my priority list is me. I must meet my relationship responsibilities to myself. Third, are my relationship responsibilities to my neighbor. Who is my neighbor? My neighbor is everyone except me! (Your list of neighbors may be extensive and unwieldy. I will address its organization later in this letter.)

Indulge me a moment as I wax poetic. Our life is like a garden. Some people have a real connection with their vegetable gardens, and others are very fond of their flower gardens. I have always found great joy and a sweet solace in orchards with lovely thick green carpets of grass. Whatever your interpretation of a garden, imagine it now in your mind. Walk into your beautiful garden and breathe in its fragrant aroma. This scenery is your life. Whatever is pleasing to you is in this place. You can add anything you wish to make it even more delightful. Inevitably, there will be some things in your garden which are not part of your design, or perhaps some things have withered; you can remove these things. Maybe they are weeds which have silently crept up, or maybe there are things brought in by someone other than you. You may remove these things. Such is your life. The New Testament reads:

> "…And now, dear brothers and sisters, one final thing. Fix your thoughts on what is true, and honorable, and right, and pure, and lovely, and admirable. Think about things that are excellent and worthy of praise."

> (Bible, Philippians chapter 4, verse 8)

If you plant these things in your garden, then you will reap a beautiful bouquet, a bouquet of love, joy, peace, patience, kindness, goodness, faithfulness, gentleness, and self-control. This bouquet is your life.

Plant this in your garden.
We are to show mercy
Plant this in your garden.
We are to make the most of every opportunity,
and we are to be happy.
Plant this in your garden.
We are to bear each other's burdens,
and we are to be unpolluted by the world.
Plant this in your garden.
We are to sing and make music in our hearts unto the Lord,
and we are to be wise.
Plant this in your garden.
We are to study the words of God,
and we are to be filled with the Holy Spirit.
Plant this in your garden.

We are to love our neighbors,
and we are to be eager to do good works always.
Plant this in your garden.
We are to pray often.
Plant this in your garden.

— Dad.

God is good! What is the burden He places on us? What stranglehold does He wish to put on us, and what is the control of our lives He desires? Is He tyrannical wrecking Men's lives? He commands us to love Him and to do good things with our lives! What a high honor this is for the Creator of everything to want, not only a connection with us but a loving relationship in which he promises us, direction, instruction, and assistance, as well as food, clothing, and shelter. But wait, there's more! He also has given us His words and a credit card with no limits in the spiritual economy courtesy Jesus the Christ and a ready-made family of fellow believers in the Church. Johnny, tell Tera what else she gets just for playing the game of life hosted by the heavenly Father. Alright, Jim, as a Christian, she will also receive the indwelling of the Holy Spirit (the third part of the God ternary) as her assistant for the remainder of her natural life. Back to you, Jim. Thank you, Johnny. Hey Johnny, you're single, right? Maybe you and Tera should go for coffee!?

That is enough of this silliness. Seriously, if you consider what He asks of us and what He will do for us (and I did not even mention the heavenly retirement plan yet), it's a no-brainer.

So, what to do? You have specific talents given to you by God when you were born. I see you have inherited some predispositions from your mother and me. I am not sure if I should say congratulations or if I should apologize. Sorry for the teeth, but maybe the mind will offset the genetic imbalance. Unique talents have been given to all, and they are as unique as fingerprints, eyes, and faces. Of all the 108,456,367,669[1] people who have ever existed, your thoughts and personality have never graced this stage of life. As with freedom, so it is with talents, there comes great responsibility and honor. You can do for the world what has never been done before and cannot ever be done again once you leave this act.

My admonition to you is simple; be kind to yourself. Take care of your body and use it for the purposes it was designed. Exercise and eat well; enjoy life! Do all things in moderation and avoid becoming a slave to anything or anyone. Use your mind as it was intended. Observe the beauty which is all around us in nature and people and art and music and literature. Never stop learning, as it will keep you young. Practice random acts of kindness and senseless acts of beauty as the bumper stickers suggest.

Most importantly, always walk with God, for he is the only constant in this place. May you always be healthy and happy. By healthy and happy, I mean take this prescription for life Health- the proper functioning of systems by their intended purpose.

Remember, "There are no perfect men just men with perfect intentions."[2] It is a matter of expedience and a requirement of survival to make certain judgments when you meet people. If a person is struggling with making their way in this world and they have made some poor choices, you will need to judge if they have perfect intentions and simply are burdened with human frailty, or if they do not like our Father. It is especially true when choosing a spouse. But I am getting ahead of myself.

INSTITUTIONAL

Chapter 14

Relationship with Your Spouse

Una mujer ejemplar, ¿quién la encontrará?
¡Vale mucho más que las piedras preciosas!
— Biblia, Proverbios 31 versículo 10.

A wife of noble character who can find? She is
worth far more than rubies:
— Bible, Proverbs, chapter 31, verse 10.

There was a tender old King who was alone, and he
had a beautiful daughter, a Princess. She had grown
in grace and stature and had found favor in the eyes
of the entire kingdom, and this pleased the King. One
day the Princess told her father, the King, she has
decided to venture to a far-off land to visit friends
and to begin her own life independent of the influence
of the Imperium. Her father was decidedly sad, and
his daughter was optimistically excited. After a few
impassioned words, she quietly left, and as he bid her
farewell, he fell to his knees and prayed for her safety,
and then he wept.

When the King received reports, his beautiful child
had begun accepting suitors; he wrote her these
words:

To my most precious endeavor, my daughter, the fair,
and the lovely Princess from her humble and most
adoring father, the King,

*It is my fervent prayer; this parchment finds you well
and in good spirits and pleasant circumstances.*

*My thoughts are with you often, as are my wishes
for your security and your contentment. I have
learned of your industriousness and successes and
have received this most agreeable news with great
satisfaction, although I must confess, I was not caught
unawares because I am familiar with your attributes
and customary behavior. However, there is another
confession I must make concerning a confidential
report I have received as of late. It was with great
trepidation I have learned of your intention to accept
suitors. I do not wish your understanding clouded
of my concern in this manner, but I pray it will be
as clear as your amber eyes. It is my estimation your
character is far beyond reproach; it is the true nature
of your prospects I call into question. I do not desire
to demonstrate contempt toward your judgment
but only offer these words for your kind and astute
contemplation. It is with these humble considerations I
submit the following.*

*It is my judgment that the delicate, intimate
relationship between a Man and a Woman deserves
the utmost respect and care in both its development
and maintenance. The marriage relationship is not a
flower to place out into your public garden but instead
is a plant to be cherished in your private garden for
your enjoyment and pleasure. In the beginning, you
must cultivate the soil of your most private relationship
into a fertile bed suitable for the healthy growth of
intimacy. It is in the nursery the highest care and focus
must be given to encourage new growth. Remember,*

*daughter, some of the most dazzling seeds are the
deceptive seeds of thorny weeds once you have chosen a
fair seed for consideration, which is pleasing to the eye
avail yourself of its characteristics. If you find you have
developed a fondness for many of its traits, you must
weigh these against any of its non-desirable attributes.
If it pleases you to accept any negatives along with its
compensations, it is now appropriate to invest time
into the toil of growing love's flower. If you have chosen
well, a sturdy and beautiful flowering bush will begin
to grow. However, I implore you and your beloved to
be patient and refrain from sampling the tender young
nubs of this exquisite flora. If you let it grow as nature
has instructed and make a fidelistic commitment
to its nurturing, then you will be rewarded with a
blossoming gift that will flourish forever and provide a
peaceful oasis from the sometimes-oppressive heat of the
days living.*

*I send you my blessings and a remark of great affection
and trusting respect, your servant, your King.*

— Dad.

THE SACRED INSTITUTION OF MARRIAGE IS ANOTHER
beautiful gift from our Father, much like the Church (called
out), science and government. Despite the discouraging divorce statistics, 95% of Americans will roll the dice and take a
chance at matrimonial bliss. Currently, our country is experi-
encing the highest rate of marriage in the world[1]. Perhaps this
is due to the spiritual influence of the founding fathers of this
nation. If that is true, then maybe the 50% divorce rate in this
country is due to their corporal influence[2]. I do not know this
to be true. But I do know of clues which may lead to answers.

I think it is curious 80% of couples cite "irreconcilable differences" as the reason for the dissolution of their marriage[3]. I think the wise old King had it right when he advised his daughter in the matters of love. I noted five key points he shared in the successful negotiation of a committed relationship. He acknowledged the initial element of attraction quickly followed by learning the true nature of your victim; I mean beloved. Next, you must weigh the information you have gathered and decide if you are willing to accept this individual with warts and all (present and future). It is at this point where the disciplined effort of patience is wisely applied by giving yourself time before you make your final decision. Only a mature and discerning person will make good use of this luxury called time. If in your most honest estimation, your chosen one is worthy, it is time to make the commitment of fidelity and take the final plunge.

The 80% statistic of marriages ending because of irreconcilable differences tempts me to conclude that of the King's five points, acceptance is the most important. Still, I think they must all be equally significant; however, if the step of acceptance had been successfully negotiated, then irreconcilable differences would not be cited as the villain of a failed marriage. If it were not acceptance, then yes, there would be another reason. Marriage is a sticky wicket. A good marriage is easily spotted; it is a giant diamond. From the outside, it is breathtaking and impervious. Within the precious gem, there are many complex structures wherein lies its strength. A good marriage is breathtaking; it is a vibrant, deliberate, and labor-intensive action. There are many angles to consider, and there are many commitments to be made.

There are many good books with useful advice for the about-to-be-wed, the already married, and the just about not to be married any longer; the best of the best is still the Holy instruction manual. The marriage relationship is not very different from any other relationship in nature; the difference lies in intensity and degree. The ingredients of attraction, knowledge, acceptance, time, and commitment are the same. I think there are similar and dissimilar responsibilities. I also think the physical, emotional, intellectual, and spiritual duties between each participant are both equal and the same.

Here is a brief outline of the Bible's example of the relationship between husband and wife. The Man is the head of the Woman as the Christ is the Head of the Church. The Man was before the Woman as the Christ was before the Church. Man serves a Woman with his life as the Christ served the Church with His life. A Woman submits to Man as the Church submits to the Christ. I think a man would do well to look to the example of how the Christ behaves toward His bride the Church when considering how to behave towards his bride. Enough said? (I Corinthians chapters 7 and 11)

If you can stand it, daughter, I would like to add a few words to the sexual aspect of this brilliant jewel. Utilize your body as it was intentionally created. Use your body parts as they were intended to be used and do not use your physical parts as they were not designed to be used; this is called abuse, even perversion. Sexual union is for procreation and deepening emotional intimacy. That is all I care to say about that subject. Enjoy! (When you are married, I mean.) Only have kids if you want to be parents; all other reasons are absurd. But I am getting ahead of myself.

Chapter 15

Relationship with Your Children

*Los hijos son una alegría al corazón o hijos son
una carga al alma, es tu decisión.*
Papá.

*Children are a joy to the heart, or children are
a burden to the soul, it is your choice.*
Dad.

I HAVE NOT FINISHED LIVING THIS LIFE YET, BUT SO FAR,
raising children has been the best thing I have done. I admit
it was a tough job, but what a ride! At first glance, this may
appear to be frivolous advice, but I promise it is profound.
Do not create children if you do not want to be a parent.
When you choose to make a child, you are also choosing to
become a parent, and this is the toughest job you will ever
love (or hate). When you decide to become a parent, you
choose the purpose of your life, for a third of your adult
years. Parenting is not for the faint of heart, but for the foolhardy who think they know a better way. Realistically most
often, the decision to begin a family is less a decision and
more a reaction to our childhood. Mom and Dad tried but,
when you get right down to it, they were clueless. I could do
it better. Here is your chance to make the perfect home and
to be the perfect parent.

*Is this really happening? Is it time? Ok, let's go! It is so
cold and dark. Of course, it's raining, and it is heavy
rain and windy. Its only water, stay focused. Yuck! We*

are soaked! I'm so cold. C'mon, start…yes! Warm-up.
Come on. Turn the defrost on. Use your sleeve to wipe
off the fog. Listen to how hard the rain is hitting the
roof! Turn the wipers on. I can barely see the road. Oh
God, protect us, and don't let anything happen to this
baby. Hang in there, Honey, we'll be there in just a bit.
I love you so much. I can't even say how much I love
you! Here we are. I'm going to park the car Hun, love
ya! I will be right there. Mom and Dad

(Tuesday night, February 16, 1982.)

Oh sweetheart, are you sure you want to go there? It is such
a beautiful thing to bring a child into the world. I *almost*
wish I could do it all over again. The whole world slowed
down when you were born. There is a smell which I remember to this day; I have not forgotten that smell. Your birth
rocked my world! The night you were born, I prayed the
hardest prayer I could, and I promised God I would teach
you about Him. Your birth awoke something deep inside me
and changed me. Your birth had even a more significant effect on me than my wedding. That might be wrong in some
way, but it is the truth.

I have always felt my children were part of me. I have
thought I share with them my fabric, which wraps up this old
bag of bones. I see some of the same design in your wrapping
as in mine. I also see parts that are like your mother's linen.
Then there are parts of your covering that are not familiar
to me, and I consider these parts are your uniqueness, and
the texture is all you and I think influenced by your spirit.
The same will be true for your children. Each one of them
will be an entirely new creation like non-other before. What
a generous gift from our Father, we should feel so honored.
It is difficult for me to fathom how God could trust us this

much. We are bringing his child into this world, and it is up to us to teach this precious, tender, innocent child how to get along in this sometimes-harsh land. We are to grow this new life with love and protection and nourishing its talents, and then one fine day, we will have the privilege of introducing our charge to his or her Heavenly Father. Being a parent has been the most humbling and educational experience in my life.

If you have determined you and your spouse are of a strong moral character, stout of heart, and a bit foolhardy, then you are ready to begin your family of education (pro-creation.) "Abandon all hope ye who enter hereinto"[1] I'm just kidding! I do not intend to layout all you need to know about raising kids but were afraid to ask. I wish to share with you just a few observations. There are no shortages of parenting books I assure you; just be cautious. I believe you and your spouse will be the best judge of how to train your children, especially if your hearts align with the God of this universe. One thought that jumps to the forefront of my mind is that children are not little adults in any aspect. Their bodies do not behave like yours, and despite your most ardent efforts, you will not be successful in changing that principle. They will need what they need when they need it. They are not evil little agents set out on a mission to inconvenience you regardless of the evidence to the contrary. Their brains are like home entertainment systems. They have this big heavy, bulky unit called a head which they cannot even support on their own for a while, with a large bundle of disconnected wires dangling in their spinal column, but you cannot see that. It takes about 13 years for all these wires to connect to where they are supposed to plug in, and even then, it is not until they are in their mid-twenties all the fine-tuning is complete. This information may be disheartening; however, I did not make this up; it is just the way we are wired.

Kiddos are like little knowledge vacuum cleaners, and at first, their mouth is the sensing tool of choice. You really must watch those rug rats; they are fast and furious. And when their leg bones harden, and they get their sense of balance plugged in, then the real fun starts. Your prime directive during the first few years is, *do not lose them*. It seems they want to go, and it doesn't matter where as long as they are going. If you were able to hang on to them up to this point, then you will be witness to a miracle. When the time is full and the season is right, your little persons "poopy wire" plugs in, and they finally can sense when its time. Sure, Wall Street will reel, and the price of Pampers stock will drop, but you are past the diaper stage! I think this day warrants a celebration, as it is a rite of passage moment. (Always look for reasons to celebrate your relationships).

My philosophy for raising offspring is to have firm boundaries but place them way, way, out there. They need limits for physical safety and emotional security, but they also need room for growth. Remember, they are independent spirits, and your preferences are just that, yours. Please do not misunderstand my statement. You do not let your inexperienced children choose for themselves unconditionally; let them make their own choices in the context of your wise discretion. It is not in children to direct their steps much in the same way it is not in us adults to direct our own steps. We look to our Heavenly Father for guidance, direction, and wisdom concerning the activities of our lives. Our children do the same, even if they seem to protest (as do we). You need to respect your children but give them a chance and teach them well. And then there is the secret ingredient. If you love your kiddos, they will know it, and love like pleats in slacks covers a multitude of sins. Love is the spackle of life which fills in all the places we missed, just like grace is Jesus' spackle, which makes up for our shortcomings. Parents are not to break the spirit of the child; they are to corral it until they can care for themselves.

At this point, there is a dynamic I wish to share with you. I am not a perfect man, and I was not a perfect Father. I gave pain to my children at times through abandonment, rejection, or unrealistic expectations creating fear in my children because I was withholding my care. This fear would convert into anger toward me for my failings, but this soon became feelings of guilt because it is not possible in the eyes of children for the parent to have faults. And guilt, when full-grown, gives birth to shame, and shame delivers despair — illustrating the mechanism of transferring unhealthy cycles from generation to generation. The effects and influence will be apparent unto the third and fourth generations, so the Scriptures teach. It is my fervent prayer that you will *not* accept my junk. Praise God I am, and you will be a perfect parent because we will and have pointed our children toward Him who is perfect. We are made perfect in Him!

> You must not bow down to them or worship them,
>   for I, the LORD your God, am a jealous God who
> will not tolerate your affection for any other gods. I
> lay the sins of the parents upon their children; the
> entire family is affected—even children in the third
>   and fourth generations of those who reject me.

(Bible, Exodus chapter 20, verse 5)

Another prayer of mine is that your children and my children will grow up to become best friends. They cannot be our friends until they grow up, because that would be asking the river of life to flow backward, but what a beautiful day when they become our fellow brother or sister traveler in this world and our fellow spirit in the next. I probably sound like a broken record, but this is important to me. Recall our marked glass cylinder or pitcher we have filled with our favorite color of water when we have met the requirements of a relationship beginning with our relationship with God. The next section we filled was our self-care and then our responsibilities to our spouse, and now we have discussed our obligations to our beloved children. These are our innermost personal relationships, but we are involved in other relationships as well; consider your relationship duties toward your family of origin. But I am getting ahead of myself.

Chapter 16

Relationship with Your Extended Family

La verdad se encuentra dentro de un pequeño
y preciso compás, pero el error es inmenso
— Henry St. John,
<u>Reflexiones sobre el exilio</u> (1716).

The truth lies within a little and certain
compass, but the error is immense
— Henry St. John,
<u>Reflections upon Exile</u> (1716).

CONDOLEEZZA RICE, SECRETARY OF STATE TO THE NATIONAL Commission on Terrorist Attacks upon the United States, testified, "They have to be right once; we have to be right 100 percent of the time."[1] It is interesting that for every situation, one could imagine there is only one correct or best response, and conversely, there is seemingly an infinite number of incorrect responses. I suppose if we focused on these unfair probabilities, we could and probably would become discouraged and overwhelmed. I will exercise my free will and move forward in my discussion with you concerning the living of life.

The home you and your beloved will craft someday will be a refuge from the sometimes-harsh outside world. Within the warm fortified walls of your cocoon, your nursery will provide the ingredients and conditions required for developing your relationship with our Farther, and for growing yourself into a healthy and thriving individual. You and your spouse will combine your sturdy stock and send down a taproot deeply and soundly into the ground, ensuring access to abundant supplies of nutrients for your possible young saplings. Your home will be a home of sustenance for the body, mind, and spirit. Your home will be one of those you see on Christmas cards. What a pleasant thought, but there is more to this life.

If you want a satisfying life, if you're going to live a life full of peace and joy, if you're going to live a life in which you wake up in the morning feeling a flutter of excitement similar to how you feel on Christmas morning then, all you need to do is expand your world. Survey the world just outside your cocoon and observe your extended family or as the anthropologist says your family of origin. As an adult member of this world and with the luxurious benefit of American citizenship and the added honor of your education, with your power comes responsibility. I humbly suggest you have some responsibility for your extended family and the extended family of your spouse.

Daughter, I think it is time to discuss the in-laws as well as the out-laws. I know your focus is presently on your life and considering your family of procreation, but you must not forget your responsibilities to your extended family. These are your roots. Just because you flew the coop does not mean you have severed all ties. What it does mean is now your parents can no longer veto your will. They are no longer accountable to God for the development of your soul. Now your will, destiny, and soul are in your own hands; you are responsible to God for the care of your soul. You need to go out and buy yourself a graduated cylinder and mark God's portion and then your part and, eventually, your spouse's section and next to your children's et cetera. You are all grown up. Now I weep for you (just kidding).

"Opportunity plus ability equals responsibility." I heard this axiom many years ago and thought it was clever, so I share it with you. However, I think it is far too broad in scope to be considered a "truth." If it were a truth, then our lives would be quite a bit more complicated. However, I don't believe life has to be complicated any more than it is at present. As I have stated several times before and I repeat it here at the risk of sounding like a broken record, life is a collection of relationships with others beginning first with our God then our self, our spouse and our children. Another relationship to consider is with our extended family. If a member of our extended family has a real need that they are unable to meet, and if there is no member of their family of procreation or origin with the ability or will to assist, and we have a surplus of said lacking asset, then, it is our honor and duty to meet the need. "If someone has enough money to live well and sees a brother or sister in need but shows no compassion—how can God's love be in that person?" (Bible, 1st John chapter 3, verse 17). Here "brother" does not refer to the family; instead, it is used in the universal sense or as a fellow human.

With our full cup, we share with others, as it would be impossible and irresponsible to share from an empty cup. Choosing to share from our partially full cup would be giving sacrificially. It is a high honor and a pleasant activity to assist those in need. I can think of no other act which provides more of a sense of wellbeing and accomplishment than doing good works. It just makes me feel proud of myself! It is puzzling to me that it appears many people are seemingly terrified of doing too much good for those in need. I have personally been on the receiving end of assistance from non-profits and the Church, as you may well remember from your childhood. I was amazed, humiliated, and angered because of the interrogations I suffered at the hands of fellow Christians. I am not ignorant; many unscrupulous individuals have made it their vocation to defraud the kind-hearted.

Still, in the words of Voltaire, "It is better to risk saving a guilty man than to condemn an innocent one"[2]. It is never right to do the wrong thing, even for the right reason. "And the King will say, 'I tell you the truth when you did it to one of the least of these my brothers and sisters, you were doing it to me!"

Further, "And he will answer, 'I tell you the truth when you refused to help the least of these my brothers and sisters, you were refusing to help me." (Bible, Matthew, chapter 25, verses 40 and 45). It is not my intention to be vague here, but I wish for you to learn from these illustrations and to apply lessons learned to the many areas of your life. If you recall, "Do not judge others, and you will not be judged. Do not condemn others, or it will all come back against you. Forgive others, and you will be forgiven. Give, and you will receive. Your gift will return to you in full pressed down, shaken together to make room for more, running over, and poured into your lap. The amount you give will determine the amount you get back. For with the measure you use, it will be measured to you" (Bible, Luke chapter 6, verses 37 and 38). If the object of your assistance lacks couth, I do not believe it excuses you from offering your best effort. As Christians, we should always strive for excellence in all we do for His glory. And of course, we must remember that our blessings are not ours; we have them on loan from the One above.

I agree we are to be good stewards of what God has entrusted us, but if we are to err, it is far better to err on the side of liberality than to let a lamb of our Father's continue in need. There is no harm done in being deceived and giving aid to an immoral person. In fact, and unbeknownst to us, there may be good done for the ways of the Lord are mysterious. Now may be the time to let the other shoe drop. If we were to be slothful in our stewardship of the things given us, we would cause injury to God's little lambs. If you have an extended family member in need and they can meet their responsibilities but do not, it would be detrimental to provide for them. We must always respect the inherent dignity within each of our brothers and sisters. To assume or overtake the responsibility of anyone degrades him or her to a lower level of esteem then they deserve. This should go without saying, but unfortunately, it does not! Far too many things seem to go unsaid, and we have forgotten some necessary human consideration and etiquette.

Situations involving other members of your extended family not meeting each other's needs are sticky wickets. On the other hand, if they have the ability but lack desire, the responsibility does not fall to you directly; however, if you genuinely care for the needy family member, what are you to do? Should you sacrifice your rights and offer help to be practical, or do you hold off on the sake of principle? I believe I will leave this one up to you and your Advisor. Another scenario to consider would be a situation where an extended family member is meeting their needs or responsibilities, but you may wish to offer a welcomed assist. For example, your adult sibling has an extremely strong-willed child who requires a great deal of effort. Perhaps you have made a connection with your niece or nephew, and you suspect taking this bundle of joy into your home for an evening or a week would provide your brother and his exhausted bride a respite. I imagine this gift or a million other similar ideas would bring satisfaction to you and joy to your beneficiaries. These principles equally apply to all relationships, even communal relationships such as the local congregation of the Church. But I am getting ahead of myself.

Chapter 17

Relationship with Your Church Family

*Nuestra ciudadanía no es de este mundo y la
embajada de nuestra patria es la iglesia*
—Papá.

*Our citizenship is not of this world, and the
embassy of our homeland is the Church*
—Dad.

Baby, your family of procreation is God's nursery for
the real world. "Direct your children onto the right path, and
when they are older, they will not leave it." (Bible, Proverbs
chapter 22, verse 6). It is helpful to keep in mind Proverbs is
a book of generalizations, not commandments. Our meaning in this life comes from the fact God created us. The Bible
paints a story with very few direct commands or instructions; however, it communicates a message which transcends
human language, and this message is translated to us by the
Holy Spirit, our comforter. We are individually responsible
for interpreting the word. Jesus, the Christ and Messiah, and
Savior came to this world and entered the Holy of Holies by
going to the cross and sacrificing himself to atone, redeem-
ing us from our doom. When He arose from the grave, He
claimed the Church or the body of believers for His own.
Presently, it is through the Church He does His work and
fights the great battle against the evil one's wicked influence
in this world.

Our meaning or purpose in life is revealed to us, and
now, I wish to discuss how we accomplish the task set before

us. I know, I know, I know. I am a broken record, but humor me. The way to have meaning or achieve our purpose in life is by having a personal relationship with God, yourself, and other people; it's the whole graduated cylinder thing. By first correctly prioritizing the relationships of our life, and then meeting the responsibilities of those ties, we live a moral life. Now, why do we want to live a righteous life or a purposeful and fulfilled life? If you will recall from earlier in this letter, I remarked the Creator of this world, and all the systems of this world made things to work a certain way. When we use these systems following their intended purpose and the correct (or moral) manner, they will work efficiently. If we consider our bodies as a system and treat them the way they were intended, then we will enjoy good health. However, the converse is true. If we abuse our bodies and use them in ways they were not designed for, the result will be diminished health. This principle is equally correct and can be applied to any area of physical, emotional, intellectual, or even spiritual being. Take a moment to reflect, and you will see this is true in physics, educational settings, and religious rites. Therefore, the reason we want to lead a moral life is it affects our real happiness! There is no other way to be happy or joyous or peaceful or content, then to be healthy. If we are healthy in our body, if we are healthy in our head, if we are healthy in our heart and if we are healthy in our spirit, then we are truly happy. Remember, "If ye know these things, happy are ye if ye do them." (Bible, John chapter 13, verse 17, King James Version). And let's not forget the ethereal mathematical theorem which states, "A negative multiplied by a positive always equals a negative." The meaning in laymen's terms is, "Doing a wrong thing for the right reason is never right." The temptation to steal a loaf of bread for your starving family is to lack faith in God to keep His promises. In situations like these, it is a deception by 'you know who' to

doubt our Father's love. I know this seems to be a hard saying, and I confess I struggle with this one often. Like that
poster with the cute little kitten says, "When you get to the
end of your rope, tie a knot and hang on!"

Our family of origin is where we prepare for admission
into the world. Our family of procreation is our refuge from
the world and the training camp for our offspring. Our citizenship is in heaven, and the Church is our embassy. The
word embassy comes from the French word ambassadeur,
which refers to the office of the Ambassador. Ambassadors
are high-ranking diplomatic representatives who serve as
spokespeople for their nation's government. If one country recognizes the sovereignty of another, they generally
establish an embassy there. It is interesting the apostle Paul
thought of himself and us as ambassadors for the Christ.
We are high-ranking diplomatic representatives who serve
as spokespersons for the Christ our Lord to this foreign land
called Earth. The Church is the gathering of our spiritual
family, and the time we gather for worship and fellowship.

The Church is our next level of relationship in our
graduated cylinder of colored water. The Church is where
we corporately meet God and our brothers and sisters and
where we initiate and facilitate His work in this world. The
Church is our embassy here on earth and functions similarly
to international embassies. It is where we come to pay honor
to our heavenly Father in song and prayer; it is where we join
in communion and meditate on the sacrifice of Jesus and his
loving gift of grace; it is a time and place for coming together
and sharing our common faith, love, and joy; it is a celebration where we reflect and rejuvenate; it is our Homecoming.

I did not understand "Church" when I was a boy and
went with my mom and grandparents. It felt as if we were
invading another world or at least a strange foreign land.
I remember feeling intimidated by these gigantic pointy

building. The air inside these edifices felt thick, heavy, and reeked with odors of musty, stale bread. Many times, there would be several distinguished-looking men to greet you at the door. When entering the quiet sanctuary, my eyes were slow to adjust to the darkness. My ears would fill with soft, sad music that seemed to be floating on the warm amber colored light radiating from the stained-glass windows. The atmospheres at other churches were different but still foreign. Friendly people who wanted to know everything about you would greet us with their vigorous handshakes, shaking your whole body. The volume level in the sanctuary was a dull roar as everyone was engaged in lively conversation. Sometimes there would be a band playing music during all this milling around. To my youthful eyes and ears, Church always seemed so mysterious. Why did these people come together, and of what were they so intently talking? I knew they were speaking in English, but a codified English as best I could tell.

Childhood memories are a curious thing, but they must give way to adult realism. The Church is not a building. It is a group of people who have dedicated their entire being to the Creator and His purposes. And Tera if one day you should decide to in the words of the Apostle Peter,

Peter replied, "Each of you must repent of your sins and turn to God and be baptized in the name of Jesus Christ for the forgiveness of your sins. Then you will receive the gift of the Holy Spirit. This promise is to you, to your children, and to those far away—all who have been called by the Lord our God.

(Bible, Acts chapter 2, verses 38 and 39)

Then He will add you to the Church, and they will be your brothers and sisters becoming your second family. You will enjoy all the benefits and have all the responsibilities of the family. If any member of the family has any need they cannot meet, we got their back, and vice versa!

When Christianity first began, times were harsh. It was a popular and fast-spreading new religion, and it was very misunderstood. During this time in history, many cults and subversive groups were popping up, which challenged the Roman government and terrified many citizens. Rumors abounded everywhere, and the new Christian movement was not immune to the hysteria. The Church bore accusations of practicing ritualistic sacrificing of infants and having orgies as part of worship.

Further, the communion was thought to be a cannibalistic feast, and sermons about the new kingdom were misconstrued to be plans of revolt against the occupying Romans. In response to these rumors and misconceptions, the early Church endured vigorous persecution, and its members subjected to much violence and terrorism. Many Christians were killed or carted off to prisons in other countries. Many families were torn apart, and Christians were blackballed from the economy at all levels. During this time, multitudes of Christians fled to various parts of the world, seeking safety. Historians refer to this mass movement as the Great Christian Diaspora. A positive consequence of the persecution of Christians was the broadcasting of the "Good News" to the entire known world in 30 year's time. A negative result of the oppression was many families had been torn apart and left destitute. Especially true for families without fathers because due to cultural mores, women were hard-pressed to support a family. These times were the roots of Christian benevolence.

Consider what you are willing to do for your own family, and these are the things you are to concern yourself with regarding your Christian family as well. It would be a dishonor to our Savior and a shame on us if we neglected a member of our family in any area of life. Every member of our family should have food, clothing, and shelter at the very minimum. But why do the minimum? Remember, Jesus said, "For with the measure you use, it will be measured to you." (Bible, Luke chapter 6, verse 38.) I know I want a lot of rewards when I get to heaven, so when I help my family members, I plan to use a large measure! The same is true of emotional and intellectual needs. We need to be there for support to our brothers and sisters because life in this old world has its pitfalls. As your home is the place where you teach your kiddos how to live, the Church is the place where we show one another how to live too. The educational aspect of the Church is a serious matter. There are so many different aspects of the Church, thus creating a place for everyone.

The Church family is very similar to your own family. It is a place of refuge and a safe place for learning life skills. Moreover, it is just a nice place to enjoy the people you love. Also, like your family, the Church reaches outside itself to care for other members of our planet. The Church is God's vehicle for meeting the needs of humanity. Because we do not see God, I think we tend to consider his work more ethereal and less to do with the physical world, but that would be incorrect. Yes, God is spirit and exists in the spiritual realm, which the Bible refers to as the heavens, but this spiritual realm coexists with the physical realm we call the world. It is the spirit within us; it is the real us which interests Him so. Therefore, it is the chief objective of the Church to fulfill the will of Jesus the Christ, "...seek and save the lost."

(Bible, Luke, chapter 19, verse 10). If you look in the Yellow Pages, you will find many churches, and this can be confusing. While there is only, "…one Lord, one faith and one baptism;" (Bible, Ephesians chapter 4, verse 5), there seem to be many branches. To some people, this is a point of concern, and they insist not all these branches can be right.

A friend of mine once theorized the reason for many branches was to accommodate varying personality types. Another friend of mine postulated these offshoots were the divisive results of satanic influence. I have my theories and am only willing to hint at them by saying I believe the Church is a spiritual institution. "…Dear friends, you always followed my instructions when I was with you. And now that I am away, it is even more important. Work hard to show the results of your salvation, obeying God with deep reverence and fear. For God is working in you, giving you the desire and the power to do what pleases him.…" (Bible, Philippians chapter 2, verse 12). Sweetie, I respectfully leave this interpretation up to you.

I cannot think of a better way to "…seek and save the lost" than to reach out in genuine love and concern and meet people where there are. My meaning is to let us love them and make them Christian not, make them Christian and then love them. Remember, God loves non-Christians as much as He loves Christians. If you're driving and come across an accident, do you get out of your vehicle and start sharing the Gospel with dazed victims? Is it more appropriate to get on your cell phone and call 911 for assistance? Perhaps it is more caring to follow up and visit the victim in the hospital and make sure their immediate needs are met; their family notified, and the family gets dinner that evening? After you love them in word and deed, then you will find an opportunity to share the Gospel. Do not throw a drowning man a Bible.

Throw him a life preserver and pull him ashore, then you can hand him a Bible and probably a towel too! Maybe the Churches should open assistance centers in downtown locations or shopping malls. But I am getting ahead of myself.

COMMUNAL

Chapter 18

Relationship with Community

Nuestro vinculo más básico y común es que todos nosotros vivimos en esta tierra. Todos respiramos el mismo aire. Todos valoramos el futuro de nuestros hijos. Y somos todos mortales.
— John F. Kennedy, Discurso, la Universidad de America, Washington D.C. (June 10, 1963).

Our most basic common link is that we all inhabit this planet. We all breathe the same air. We all cherish our children's future. And we are all mortal.
—John F. Kennedy, Address, American University, Washington, D.C. (June 10, 1963).

Sugar, this may seem like an unlikely place for this discussion, but I feel it would be an appropriate topic anywhere. The mystical and mysterious creature called Man exists in three different realms. There is the apparent physical realm, here on planet Earth. There is the not so visible realm, called the spirit world. Then there is the domain of the mental/emotional field I like to refer to as the transitional terminal. This is where our spirit meets with our body, and they negotiate with one another to determine one's physical behavior. In a simple Venn diagram, the area where two circles intersect is called a subset; this subset correlates to our intersecting physical and spiritual natures. I find it very curious the Hebrew word **sub** refers to the turning from sin to righteousness (physical and spiritual behavior), with sorrow (an emotion which mirrors thought). A writer of the Old Testament Proverbs stated, "As a man thinks in his heart so is, he." (Bible, Proverbs chapter 23, verse 7a, King James Version). A lovely summation.

You may consider the above to be a parenthetical thought if you wish; however, I believe you will see it fits nicely into the following treatise. If you would be so gracious and allow me to be so bold, I would like to refresh your memory of a previous thought, which I presented earlier in this letter. The bulk of our life experience is relationships with others, including our Father. These said relationships carry inherent responsibilities that fall into three categories: the physical, emotional/mental, and spiritual realms. One's thoughts are translated through our proactive mind eliciting reflective emotions and ordering our reactive behavior. I charge on to the subject of our responsibilities to our friends and neighbors.

As a card-carrying member of the human race, we are responsible for getting along with others and playing nice. If we see our fellow playmates in need of food or clothing or shelter, and they cannot satisfy these needs, our compassion compels us to reach out to help as much as we can. The same is true for their emotional and mental needs, and most undoubtedly concerning their spiritual needs. All our interactions with others, no matter who they are, should be prefaced with respect for their dignity. Being a realist, I must remark that more times than not, we will lack the necessary resources and abilities. Therefore, we live in communities; everyone has their unique interest and talents when these combine in a community, everyone shares them, and the needs of the community can be met.

The band of the community enables us to extract a synergistic result. When two plus two equals nine. Pooling our talents and resources allows us to meet needs, which on our own, we are unable to accomplish. We can meet all our physical needs through the cooperative creation of commerce, municipalities, and non-profit organizations — with the help of gas stations and grocery stores. Not forgetting fire departments and utilities, the United Way agencies and hospitals are the result of a high degree of coordinated cooperation. Our interdependence quickly is becoming apparent! I should mention other things like our roads and parks. The Make a Wish Foundation, and public radio and TV. Where would we be without phones, railroads, ships, and airplanes? Our country has benefited from cooperation.

The Church is a subset of our community, speaking in strictly anthropological terms. The Church reaches out into society to address critical spiritual concerns, as we have previously discussed. Because the Church is in the people business, it also seeks to meet the physical and mental/emotional needs of their surrounding communities; many congregations even make international efforts.

The influence of community touches every area of our lives, not just the physical and spiritual. We must also consider counseling centers and daycare centers; these tend to the emotional and mental needs of the community; the YMCA and YWCA, and scouting organizations are other examples. The rise in the number of crisis centers has increased dramatically in response to the stress-induced pressures of modern society. We seem to all agree education is a crucial facet of human development, and this has led to free compulsory education and public schools. (I do not know if the proceeding statement bothered you, but it made my ears cringe; am I mistaken in thinking the phrase "free compulsory education" is an oxymoron? How can compulsory education be free if you take away my free will? This education cost me my free will. It is not free.)

I suppose I find it a curious thing in this land of freedom that we are as bold as to compel a significant part of the population to do anything. At the outset of our country's development, education was a private matter, and seemingly out of the blue, compulsory education was born during the mid-nineteenth century. By the turn of the 20th century, school choice had ended. I read an article by a gentleman named Rick Gee[1] who shared that the U.S. Commissioner of Education William Torrey Harris had assured railroad magnate Collis Huntington, that American schools were "scientifically designed" to prevent "over-education" from occurring. In 1896, John Dewey at the University of Chicago, said, "independent, self-reliant people were a counterproductive anachronism in the collective society of the future." Dewey went on to assert, in modern society, "people would be defined by their associations, not by their accomplishments." He further shared the goals of the Prussian state, the first to force education; it was simple then, to sort obedient soldiers to the army, subservient workers to the mines, submissive civil servants to the government, and compliant clerks to the industry. But I am getting ahead of myself.

Chapter 19

Relationship with Government

Buenos principios crean buenos fines.
— Proverbio Ingles.

Good beginnings make for good endings.
— English Proverb.

OUR BEGINNINGS WERE HUMBLE, INDEED! THERE WERE several attempts by the English to settle the new world. But not until November 1620, when 102 pilgrims from England and Holland seeking a new land where they could openly practice their religious beliefs arrived, did they permanently settle in what is today called Plymouth, Massachusetts. And when it came time to separate ourselves from the perceived tyrannical rule of the British crown, it was accomplished by the authority of 'Nature,' 'Nature's God,' 'Man's Creator,' 'Supreme Judge,' and 'under Divine Providence' extracting from the Declaration of Independence. If our government fails to provide as we expect, it is the right of the people to alter or abolish it and establish a new government. I think it is safe to say while the founding fathers acknowledged God gave the right to self-government, they also felt the government should not become involved in religious issues or activities (let us remember that a church-state government had recently burned them).

It is essential to note the first amendment to the constitution states the government cannot become involved in the establishing of religion or prohibiting the free exercise thereof. The purpose of the constitution was "in Order to form a more perfect Union, establish Justice, insure domestic Tranquility, provide for the common defence, promote the general Welfare, and secure the Blessings of Liberty to ourselves and our Posterity, do ordain and establish this Constitution for the United States of America." The first of its settlers were indeed seeking religious freedom, and the framers of the constitution were intent on not allowing the government to play any role in religion or permit the government to inhibit the free practice of religion. I recall Jesus standing before the Roman law, and it found no guilt in Him. However, a few sects of the Jews persisted, claiming he had broken their religious law. Paul wrote there are no governments except those established by God, and these governments are not to be feared if you do what is right. If our government begins to make religious rules, then we have something to fear. What if these new laws are not based on "our" religion? Christian men who had some Christian values founded the USA, and they wisely incorporated some of these values into our form of government. However, they had learned from experience that using religion to govern a vast population violates the fundamental right for everyone "…to work out your salvation…" (Bible, Philippians chapter 2, verse 12), individually and choose the lifestyle which leads thereunto. History has taught us the government should mind its own business, and religions should do the same. It is inappropriate for somebody, or a group of somebodies, to suggest utilizing governmental systems to enforce their selected value system or ideas. Imagine what it would be like if someone else's flavor of values came into a position of influence in our government. The political arena is not the appropriate venue for disusing and settling religious issues, or any moral dilemmas, any more than the local church, is the proper place for discussing the restructuring of tax codes. Do you recall when the Pharisees were attempting to set up

Jesus and to get Him to incriminate himself? They presented a political issue into the spiritual arena. They asked Him His opinion,

> Now tell us what you think about this: "Is it right
> to pay taxes to Caesar or not?"

> But Jesus knew their evil motives. "You hypocrites!"
> he said. "Why are you trying to trap me? Here,
> show me the coin used for the tax." When they
> handed him a Roman coin, he asked, "Whose
> picture and title are stamped on it?"

> "Caesar's," they replied.

> "Well, then," he said, "give to Caesar what belongs
> to Caesar, and give to God what belongs to God."

> (Bible, Matthew, chapter 22, verses 17-21)

Effectively, Jesus separated Church and State. As Thomas Jefferson stated in a letter,

> "Believing with you that religion is a matter which
> lies solely between Man and his God; that he owes
> account to none other for his faith or his worship;
> that the legislative powers of government reach
> actions only and not opinions, I contemplate with
> sovereign reverence that act of the whole American
> people which declared that their legislature should
> 'make no law respecting an establishment of reli-
> gion or prohibiting the free exercise thereof,' thus
> building a wall of separation between Church and
> State."[1]

The above comments suggest our government desired God's influence, but they did not want the government's control over religion. Benjamin Franklin strongly recommended, "assistance of Heaven and its blessings sought each morning, and clergy brought in to officiate in that service."[2] This tradition continues to this very day. Careful observation demonstrates this wall of separation has a one-way door that desires Supernatural assistance to enter our politics but does not allow politics to exit into our religion. John Adams stated, "Our Constitution was made only for a moral and religious people. It is wholly inadequate to the government of any other."[3]

God establishes governments. It is His gift to humankind like the gift of science. The government is merely a tool benefiting us security from other hostile countries and other hostile compatriots. Beyond that, if we are so inclined as a people, we may use the structure of the government to meet the additional humanitarian and utilitarian needs of our fellows. While municipalities are well suited for meeting many of our physical needs, it is the Church that is suited for meeting our spiritual needs. The service government provides to the governed is the protection of their assumed individual rights to safety, peace, and the freedom to pursue happiness. The realm of governmental influence is where there is an interaction between and within its citizenry. It is my assertion private individual activities that do not involve human interaction are not subject to Man's law; we have a right to privacy. The function of the government is not the enforcement of a particular form of Christianity; however, our laws do reflect the moral climate of a country. "The law is the witness and external deposit of our moral life. Its history is the history of the moral development of the race."[4,5]

I agree the greatness of this country has been, and hopefully will continue to be, our adherence to Christian values patterned into our form of government. I do not purpose or support deleting any of these from our laws, rules of government, our foundational education system, or from our time-honored cultural traditions. Christian values like freedom, equality, justice, compassion, tolerance, forgiveness, respect, industriousness, and responsibility are indispensable foundations for our governance. I hope the Bible will heavily influence the laws of society where I live, and I hope no government will try to regulate my thought or private action. The facts are 98% of our political forefathers were Christian; they desired Heavenly guidance and arranged for clerical intercession, and they acted to prevent governmental intrusion into religion. An additional fact is 86% of U.S. citizens consider themselves Christian. If the majority of a county's citizens are Christians, does that make the country a Christian nation? If so, then we are a Christian nation. If our form of government was given to us by Jesus, the Christ that would make us a Christian government, but it was not. As I recall, Jesus was adamant his kingdom was not of this world. I further remember God has established all governing authorities, which does not mean they are all godly.

So how does a modern-day U.S. Christian interact with their government? Since our citizenship is in heaven, are we precluded from being involved in politics? Do we have any responsibilities in this area? What can we do? Do Christians have a duty to influence the government to pass laws that are consistent with our values? It is in our Church and home where we busy ourselves with matters of the soul. It is in this arena we consider worship, fellowship, growth, and evangelism. The Church is our refuge, our retreat, our quiet and safe place. Dare I say it? The Church is God's tool for doing His work. So, how does the modern-day U.S. Christian interact with their government? In the same manner, they interact with all other areas of their life, as Jesus did. (Remember the WWJD bracelets? What Would Jesus Do?) The indwelling of the Holy Spirit influences everything we do. We are affected in all areas of our existence. When we vote, when we go to the doctor, when we go to school, when we eat, when we play, no matter where we go or what we do, our behavior is shaded by our love for and our devotion to God. When spiritual issues do arise in the political sphere, it is a **good** thing to respond in a Christ-like way. But if we want to seek and save the lost, it is an even **better** thing to do this in the spiritual sphere. It is better to create a 'desire' to do good than to create a 'requirement' to do good. In other more grammatically correct words, I believe if a follower of the Christ and a servant of our Father wishes to inspire and encourage others to be in harmony with His way, they would do better and be more successful in communicating on an individual basis then through the impersonal venue of legislation. After all, morality is a private issue between the individual and God.

I conclude that based on the comments mentioned above of our countrymen and our Lord Jesus the Christ and God himself, we can bring our morality with us in all our endeavors, including political ones. Still, we can never utilize politics to govern our morality or other religious expressions and exercise. The function of the government is to protect our peace, life, freedom, and our pursuit of happiness; it is not the enforcement of a form of Christianity. Our land would benefit if all those who enter the noble vocation of public administration or military service were of the highest ethical character. It seems all major governments have exerted themselves out of a systematic belief system coupled with spiritual motivations. At first glance, it may appear religion and government a bad idea since all governments eventually fail their citizenry, but it is not the government or religion which fails. It is always those *entrusted with the administration of government* who are drawn away by their evil desires. When the opportunity presents itself, they pounce like a famine-starved tiger who luckily stumbled upon fresh prey. The sweet smell of the blood of money and power is difficult to resist, especially for those who are starving from a diet low in spiritual sustenance. It is my opinion that the confidently nourished and well-exercised spiritually as well as mentally and physically are good candidates for office. How delightful it would be if we could whole-heartedly support and depend on our government and how wonderful it would be if the international community could trust us to behave consistently, ethically, and compassionately. But I am getting ahead of myself.

Chapter 20

Relationship with International Community

*¿Por qué te fijas en la astilla que tiene tu
hermano en el ojo, y no le das importancia
a la viga que está en el tuyo? ¿Cómo puedes
decirle a tu hermano: "Déjame sacarte la
astilla del ojo", cuando ahí tienes una viga en
el tuyo? ¡Hipócrita!, saca primero la viga de tu
propio ojo, y entonces verás con claridad para
sacar la astilla del ojo de tu hermano.-*
—Biblia, Mateo 7 versículos 3-5.

*Why do you look at the speck of sawdust in
your brother's eye and pay no attention to the
plank in your own eye? How can you say to
your brother, 'let me take the speck out of your
eye,' when all the time there is a plank in your
own eye? You hypocrite first take the plank out
of your own eye, and then you will see clearly
to remove the speck from your brother's eye.*
— Bible, Matthew, chapter 7, verses 3-5.

It is good to remember these words from Jesus as I
begin to discuss our responsibilities as a nation. To the
international community, the United States Government is
Christianity. Part of the reason for our nation's unpopularity
is because of perceived hypocrisy. Our government does not
always behave in a Christ-like manner.

Perhaps it is a good idea to take a personal inventory
before we begin to assist others. I believe I have shown you

there is a hierarchy of duties conferred upon humankind, just as there are several privileges given to humans at conception. I have explained these responsibilities must be met in their order of importance. There is no difference if we are speaking of an individual or a nation. As a nation, we must first consider our present state of affairs. We are rich, we are sophisticated, and we are even beautiful as a State in the community of other nations. We are the richest and the most powerful; therefore, we assume international responsibilities. Whoa, cowboy! Before the U.S. of A. goes out into the world slinging its good influence, we had better make sure all our family has everything they need. What sense would it make for the U.S. to help some country dig water wells when back home our families are suffering because they lack water?

We must be meeting our internal needs as a nation reasonably well before we go gallivanting off to the four corners of the world, showing off our good fortune. The arrival of the international community is a new phenomenon brought on by the industrial revolution. The world is no longer this unfathomable and hostile giant. The world began to shrink in the mid-18th century and continues to do so to this present day. The analogy of the international neighborhood has never been more appropriate than it is today. As a respectable citizen of this neighborhood, we naturally desire to do our part in making this the best area possible. However, if our cup is empty or nearly empty what do, we have to offer to our international friends? It behooves us to first take care of business at home before extending a helping hand to others. You cannot share what you do not have. Have you ever heard of the Preacher's Kid Syndrome? The preacher spends so much time caring for his congregation that he neglects his own family, and his children grow up to be the bane of society. It would be shameful for our country to ignore the needs of its citizens while putting on a good face for the neighbors to see.

It seems the advent of the industrial revolution and the resultant shrinking world precipitated the need for acknowledging our neighbors and admitting that their state of being holds sway over our state of being to a degree. There has arisen a new concept for the first time in history. This new concept is an international responsibility. One of the early international discussions was the Geneva Convention.[1] The topic of discussion was an ancient one concerning the treatment of prisoners of war; however, it was the scope of participants that set a new precedent in 1863. In 1863 12 nations signed this document, and in 1949 there were 196 signers. This convention has convened seven times since the inaugural session for updating its resolutions. The Red Cross is the chief drafter and enforcer of the convention's resolutions. (Cultural sensitivity necessitated four other names: Red Lion with Sun, Red Shield of David, Red Crescent and Red Crystal.)

The most significant entity to arise out of this new global conscientious, in my opinion, was the United Nations[2] in 1945 just after World War II in San Francisco. Initially, there were 50-member countries, and now there are 193.[3] Reading the Charter of the United Nations[4] made me feel proud to be a member of humanity and increased my level of optimism for our capacity to work together and make a positive impact within the international community. In the Charter, there is a presupposition that addresses the obligation of the individual state to meet the needs of its people as well as its duties to the international community. Further, the charter acknowledges, "…that it cannot be assumed that every State will always be able, or willing, to meet its responsibilities to protect its people and avoid harming its neighbors." In these circumstances, the community rallies behind that country in support and donates necessary capacities and supplies. Three years later, the United Nations ratified the Universal Declaration of Human Rights.[5]

Again, I was overcome with emotion and proud of us as a species for producing such a beautiful document.

I remember as young men hearing then-Governor Jimmy Carter's comment, the purpose of government was to make it easy for people to do good and to make it difficult for people to do evil.[6] I would have to agree with that statement even though it is a rather broad and general one. I think the function of government is to serve its master (us) and provide what we require for our collective well-being. I have already discussed the government is to provide security through civil and international law. Also, to provide physical protection by raising and maintaining a military force. It is to establish a network of finance and commerce. However, it can do more, and we have elected to utilize this resource to provide other functions. We created a tool for dealing with homeland poverty due to family break down or physical impairment. We combined resources to develop the most successful agricultural industry in the world. This listing could go on and on, but I think you get the idea.

The other side of the coin is not so pretty. Currently, there is a whole generation of disenfranchised, disillusioned, and overwhelmed youth because we lied to them, saying that they could do anything they wished and that they would be successful. We feed them with stories of how we are the greatest nation on earth, and no one could hurt us. By example, we have imparted arrogance to our successors, which will not serve them well in their future participation within the global community. This new generation is under the false impression we are above the rules because of our lofty status worldwide. We must teach them freedom is freedom from tyranny, not freedom from responsibility, and decency. In

1999, the General Assembly of the United Nations adopted resolution 53/144 entitled <u>Declaration on the Rights and Responsibility of Individuals, Groups, and Organs of Society to Promote and Protect Universally Recognized Human Rights and Fundamental Freedoms.</u>[7] In effect, this was a reaffirmation of the 1948 <u>Universal Declaration of Human Rights</u> but with teeth. They not only listed human rights but also indicated the implied actions necessary for compliance. One line of the March 8, 1999 document intrigued me. They felt compelled to state explicitly, "...the absence of international peace and security does not excuse noncompliance." Human rights and the appropriate treatment of humans is always right regardless of the circumstances. Right is always right!

If we as a nation desire to take a leadership role in the international community, we must first remove the plank in our eye, and then with respect and dignity, we may begin to remove the sawdust from our neighbor's eye. We must bring our national convictions with us when we minister to others. We must share Voltaire's attitude of tolerance when he declared, "I disapprove of what you say, but I will defend to the death your right to say it."[8] Tolerance is not accepting another's points of view. It is respecting another's free will. When we help an individual or a nation, we are not helping them to change them. We are helping them because they need help. I am not naive to the reality we will never completely resolve all the woes we suffer, but we must do better.

Sometimes emergencies change our priorities temporarily, but 16% of our citizenry living in poverty is unacceptable. Violent offenders victimize over 10% of our population every year. Our prisons are holding about 1% of the total population of this country, costing taxpayers over 1 billion dollars annually. 70% of inmates are black, while 12% of this country's population is black. The average white family has $88,000.00 in net assets, while the average black family has $5,800.00 in net assets. Estimates demonstrate due to equipment failure, 10% of cast ballots go uncounted. It strikes me as odd 1% of Americans control over 33% of our nation's wealth. 39% of working Americans do not have any form of health insurance. 78% of US women are physically victimized at least once in their life, and 79% of women have been sexually victimized at least once in their life.[9]

Although illegal, US personnel have tortured many prisoners on many occasions. It is embarrassing when the State Department releases its annual <u>Country Reports on Human Rights Practices,</u>[10] which comments on the misdeeds of more than 190 countries and conveniently does not comment on the United States' dirty laundry.

I am not trying to bash my **precious, beautiful country;** instead, I want to make us aware of how we are living up to the <u>Ugly American</u>[11] perception so many of our neighbors hold. While it is true, I am mostly concerned with the home front, I still feel as a nation we have a responsibility to the rest of the international community. If I have an obligation to my neighbors, then my country has an obligation to its neighbors. In the same manner, I care for the needs of my neighbor; the state should feel a responsibility to meet the needs of its neighbors.

In the same way, our local communities join to combine talents and resources and reaches out to those in need; our country should organize in a manner befitting our honorable standing in the international community.

It does not matter if you are an individual, a group, or an organization or if you are an entire nation, you should always do unto others, as you would have them do unto you. Amazingly, some people in government leadership think there is a different set of rules for international interaction. I am aware it seems we are living in uniquely dangerous times, but if you consider for a moment every generation since the inception of our country has felt the same way. Things change, but they are always the same. We must be diligent and responsible but not at the expense of our morality. It is never right to do the wrong thing for the right reason. I, too, have been tempted to call myself utilitarian and walk on that slippery slope for my most noble cause. If my family is starving, do I have the right, nay, the duty to steal a loaf of bread? Here the men are separated from the boys. It will take moral courage. Having faith in God steels a man's nerves and puts iron in his backbone.[12] I do not have the right to steal. No one has the right to sin. Our Father promised we would always have food, clothing, and shelter. And if not? Heaven is not such a bad alternative. If we bend the rules or even break the rules for a good cause, we are failing to trust our Father. We are taking matters into our own hands, and that is the sin of the pride of life or playing God.

Remember, the same guidelines we use when helping our neighbor at home also apply when one nation assists another. We must always remember to treat others with respect their spirit deserves because of its heavenly origins. When you help a neighbor, you let them do what they can, and then you step in and fill in what is missing. You would not tell your neighbor what color to paint his bedroom, and we should not presume to direct our international friends how to paint their bedrooms either. Just because we decide to help someone, it doesn't mean all the rules of the universe change. Think about it, do you want to be responsible for your neighbor? It is difficult enough just being responsible for oneself, thank you very much!

There are many ways to be helpful to our neighbors. It is a simple matter to meet physical needs. Send some food or give them some money, no sweat. Tending to the intellectual and emotional deficits of a country can pose a more formable challenge. Not only do these situations require more deliberate action, but they also demand a commitment of time. It is not surprising we are called ugly Americans. What is the message we are sending when we help people the way we think they should be supported rather than the way they know they need help? When we deliver a starving country a container full of stuffed animals and teddy bears, I am reminded of the improbable story how the French peasants felt when they heard Marie Antoinette's infamous quote of "Let them eat cake."[13] If this story were true, (many think it is not) one can only imagine the anger of the starving French.

We must be wise in all our ways of dealing with fellow humans. If our country is concerned with the spiritual needs of a neighbor, it should defer to the many churches which are more than willing and very capable of filling the need. As a nation, we are not excused from good manners or good morality. The rules of individual behavior, which we all learned in kindergarten, are the rules for national conduct. If we promise to provide protection, then we should do it. If we made the decision not to use torture, then let us not send prisoners to other countries for interrogation and torture. And if we don't want bad guys to be able to buy technical weaponry to attack us, then we should not sell technological weaponry to guys with chips on their shoulders. It just does not make any sense. We should trust God enough to treat all other nations the way we want them to treat us. After all, we are all brothers in the game of life. But I am getting ahead of myself.

* * *

Christmas Truce: The Western Front 1914

THE CHRISTMAS TRUCE OF 1914 HAPPENED. IT IS AS MUCH a part of the historical texture of World War I as the gas clouds of Ypres or the Battle of the Somme or the Armistice of 1918. Yet it has often been dismissed as though it were merely a myth. Or, assuming anything of the kind occurred, it has been a minor incident, blown up out of all proportion, natural fodder for sentimentalists and pacifists of later generations.

But the truce did take place, and on some far greater scale than has been generally realized. Enemy met enemy between the trenches. There was for a time, genuine peace in No Man's Land. Though Germans and British were the main participants, French and Belgians took part as well. Most of those involved agreed it was a remarkable way to spend Christmas. "Just you think," wrote one British soldier, "that while you were eating your turkey, etc., I was out talking and shaking hands with the very men I had been trying to kill a few hours before! It was astounding!"

"It was a day of peace in war," commented a German participant, "It is only a pity that it was not decisive peace."

So, the Christmas Truce is no legend. It is not surprising, however, given the standard popular perception of World War I, that this supreme instance of "All Quiet on the Western Front" has come to have something of legendary quality. People, who would normally dismiss that far off conflict of their grandfathers in the century's teens as merely incomprehensible, find reassurance, even a kind of hope, in the Christmas truce.

This was not, however, a unique occurrence in the history of war. Though it surprised people at the time - and continues to do so today - it was a resurgence of a long-established tradition.

Informal truces and small armistices have often taken place during prolonged periods of fighting and the military history of the last two centuries abounds with incidents of friendship between enemies.

In the Peninsula War, British and French Troops at times visited each other's lines, drew water at the same wells, and even sat around the same campfire sharing their rations and playing cards.

In the Crimean War, British, French, and Russians at quiet times also gathered around the same fire, smoking, and drinking. In the American Civil War Yankees and Rebels traded tobacco, coffee, and newspapers fished peacefully on opposite sides of the same stream and even collected wild blackberries together. Similar stories are told of the Boer War, in which, on one occasion, during a conference of commanders, the rank and file of both sides engaged in a friendly game of football.

Later wars, too, have their small crop of such stories. It is rare for conflict at close quarters to continue very long without some generous gestures between enemies or an upsurge in the 'live and let live' spirit. So, the Christmas truce of 1914 does not stand alone; on the other hand, it is undoubtedly the greatest example of its kind.

There are certain misapprehensions regarding the Christmas truce. One widely held assumption is that only ordinary soldiers took part in it; that it was, as it were, essentially a protest of cannon-fodder, Private Tommy and Musketeer Fritz throwing aside the assumptions of conventional nationalism and thumbing their noses at those in authority over them.

In fact, in many cases, NCOs and officers joined in with equal readiness. At the same time, other truces were initiated, and the terms of armistice agreed at 'parleys' of officers between the trenches.

There is also some evidence that while some generals angrily opposed the truce, others tolerated it and indeed saw some advantage in allowing events to take their own course while never for a moment doubting that eventually, the war would resume in full earnest.

One other misapprehension about the truce calls for a rebuttal. There has grown up a belief, even among aficionados of World War I, that the Christmas truce was so disgraceful and event, one so against the prevailing mood of the time, that all knowledge of it was withheld from the public at home until the war was over.

The truce was fully publicized from the moment news of it reached home. Throughout January 1915 numerous local and national newspapers in Britain printed letter after letter from soldiers who took part; also, they ran eye-catching headlines ("Extraordinary Unofficial Armistice," "British, Indians, and Germans shake hands"), and even printed photographs of the Britons and Germans in No Man's Land. Germany also gave the event press publicity, though on a smaller scale and for a shorter period.

Publishing a year later, Sir Arthur Conan Doyle in his history of 1914 called the Christmas truce "an amazing spectacle" and in a memorable description, saluted it as "one human episode amid all the atrocities which have stained the memory of the war."

The phrase sums up the attraction of the truce: it is the human dimension which means that this relatively obscure event in the fifth month of a 52-month war is still remembered and will continue to catch the imagination.

In a century in which our conception of war has changed fundamentally, from the cavalry charge and the flash of sabers to the Exocet, the cruise missile and the Trident submarine, the fact that in 1914 some thousands of the fighting men of the belligerent nations met and shook hands between their trenches strikes a powerful and appealing note. It is perhaps the best and most heartening Christmas story of modern times.[14]

Chapter 21

Relationship with E.T.

¿Hay otras personas allá en el universo? ...Si solo somos nosotros, me parece un malgaste de espacio. Conversación entre el carácter de Jodie Foster y lo de Diego Montoya en la película, Contact (1997).

Are there other people out there in the universe? ....If it's just us, seems like an awful waste of space. A conversation between Jodie Foster's and Diego Montoya's charters in the film, Contact (1997).

I HAVE HAD THE PRIVILEGE OF STANDING ON THE SHORE OF Lake Almanor in Northern California at the end of summer at about midnight. I stood in the cold water and felt the crisp air flap my hair. I gazed up at the clear black sky, and it's suspended diamonds which seemed close enough to pluck and place in your pocket. I wish you could have been there with me. I saw a shooting star, and it set me to thinking there sure is a lot of space up there. I thought, why is there so much unused space, or is it being used, and we don't know about it? Why have there been so many reports of alien abductions and contacts? I read there have been 140 million of these events in modern times.

Do you remember hearing of those large pictures made of stones laid out on the ground in Peru?[1] They are so huge you can only view them from an airplane. Is it not strange when you consider there were no means of ascending to the altitude necessary for viewing?

Further, ponder the phenomenon of pyramids. Pyramids have been found in Egypt, Spain, South America, China, and Thailand, and even in Russia. I do not know if you remember, but we visited Pinson mounds in Tennessee and saw these pyramid-shaped mounds used for ceremonies and burials 1,500 hundred years before the arrival of Native Americans. We never did make it to the Mississippi pyramids. Something was going on several thousand years ago, but I haven't a clue what.

I know this sounds fantastic, but there are even more stories. Former President Jimmy Carter spoke of an experience of his in which he witnessed a UFO.[2] When he ran for the presidency, one of his platform pledges was to release classified government documents about UFO activity and interaction with our military. While serving as President, he requested the Rand Corporation (a California think tank) to investigate the phenomena. Soon after undertaking the request, certain unidentified Pentagon officials bluntly indicated if the researchers at Rand did not cease all investigations, the Department of Defense would cancel all their contracts. Because the bulk of Rand's business is with the DOD, they complied. All UFO studies were suspended. The Department's official position is they are unaware of any extraterrestrial life.[3]

The General Assembly of the United Nations reacted to a report stating there is enough scientific evidence to warrant the formation of a council. This council would study the extraterrestrial evidence, monitor new information, and make reports to the Sectary-General. An agreement was reached on December 18, 1978. Still, no further action has ever been taken.[4] The United Nations does, however, sponsor the UN Society for Enlightenment and Transformation.[5]

This sanctioned group devotes itself to the discussion of the global implications of the interaction between the community of earth and extraterrestrials. It seems there are more people than I suspected taking this subject quite seriously.

If we do have E.T. neighbors visiting us, then I suppose it follows we have responsibilities to them as well. If they require any assistance with physical needs and we have the ability, then we are obligated to comply. The same would be true of emotional and intellectual needs. Addressing spiritual needs would be a bit more complicated. Is it possible our Father will have a different system of interaction with them than He does with us here on Earth? Discussions with the aliens on this topic would be fascinating. The international community, except for spiritual issues, would appropriately undertake the above task. The Church would most appropriately address the later point.

I am not convinced E.T. exists, but if he does, then we are covered. As the old saying goes, "The only thing you can be certain of is death and taxes." But I am getting ahead of myself.

SECTION 4

WHAT IS NEXT

Chapter 22

Death and Beyond

*La muerte nunca llega a tiempo. O llega
demasiado temprano o llega demasiado tarde.*
— Proverbio Ingles.

*Death never arrives on time. It either arrives
too early, or it arrives too late.*
— English Proverb.

SOME PEOPLE SAY WITHOUT DEATH, LIFE WOULD BE
meaningless. I don't think I would go that far, but I do think
I get their meaning. Some see their impending demise as
a motivator to live life; again, I see their point, but I still
think something is missing. It seems fashionable these days
to embrace death as a noble end to a well-lived life. To me,
it just does not sound natural. Death is a bad thing, and we
should avoid it at all costs, and it should never be invited.
Death is our enemy from the day we are born. "Do not go
gentle into that good night, Old age should burn and rave
at close of day; Rage, rage against the dying of the light."[1]
We were not created to die; we were created to live forever.
The only reason we die is that Adam and Eve sinned when
they ate of the tree God said, "...You are free to eat from any
tree in the garden; but you must not eat from the tree of the
knowledge of good and evil, for when you eat of it, you will
surely die." (Bible, Genesis chapter 2 verses 16 and 17.) Ever
since then, people have been dying.

Death is a dire thing, and I think you must have a clear
understanding of what it is and what it means. "I knew you

before I formed you in your mother's womb. Before you were born, I set you apart and appointed you as my prophet to the nations." (Bible, Jeremiah chapter 1, verse 5.) He knew your predispositions. He knew your mix of DNA. He knew what genes you would inherit from your mother and me. The only thing he didn't know is what choices you would make during your life or if you would choose Him. That was because of His gift of free will to you from Him through me. I just had to include myself in there somewhere. Now you find yourself living life as you should, and this is as it should be.

Nevertheless, you will notice some disturbing things along your way. You may, at some point, find your body can, at times, behave in a most disagreeable way. Being a female as you are, there seem to be many parts that can cease working properly — an example of what is called the fallen state of Man. Now, Adam and Eve sinned; evil entered this world. Somehow and I don't understand it, but the curse put rocks in the dirt and weeds in the fields and made sweet sugar the favorite food of bacteria. It turned all my favorite foods into junk food or high in fats. When I fall, it hurts, and that is just not right. Since evil turned my hair gray, good sleep escapes me, and I am urgently awakened several times nightly. I understand a baby grows into a child and then an adult, but I cannot understand why an adult must turn into a senior. I know it is because evil has entered the world. Maybe that is why death seems so opposite of how things should be.

We were made to live forever, but because of evil, we do not get to live forever. Therefore, it is so important to have a good relationship with our Father because He is The God who made this world and everything in it, including you and me. He saw what Adam and Eve did, and he knew the consequences. As soon as he became aware of evil entering the world, and even before it came, He had a plan for defeating the evil. Evil is satan, and he thinks that by bringing death into the world, he can destroy what God loves. But the devil is wrong; God had a plan for this turn of events begun by the first humans. The idea was a drastic plan requiring the pure blood of His Son Jesus. This plan is now in action, and death is not the end of the road.

When my sorry old bag of bones gives out, and I hope it isn't too far in the future, God's breath of life will return to Him, my soul will go to sleep, and my body will return to the earth. Then maybe I will finally get some good uninterrupted sleep. Now there, Honey, things are not as bleak as they seem. I suppose now would be a good time to tell you about the plan God and His Son Jesus worked out eons ago. Because God is just, he could not excuse sin. There was a price to redeem one who had sinned, and the price was death. The plan, which is called the "Good News" or "Gospel," is Jesus would become a human and live a sin-free life. Therefore, his death would qualify as the redemptive payment for the sin of all humanity. But there is more. The plan has some stipulations.

The plan pertains to every human who ever was, is, or will be. All anyone must do is have faith and repent of your sin and keep the commandments of Jesus Christ for the forgiveness of your sins (obedience is the natural consequence of your love for Him). You will arise from the water, a new creature. What kind of new creature will you be? On the outside, you will look the same except wet from baptism, but on the inside, your soul will be white as snow, and you will be a Christian. You will have the same breath of God you always had, but now you will also have the Holy Spirit in you too. The Holy Spirit is God's presence with you, He will teach you about God's truth by the Word, and he will comfort you when you are troubled, and He will guide you in the choices you will make. Do not make the mistake of thinking the Holy Spirit will somehow impinge your free will; it will not. The Holy Spirit is at your disposal and offers protection from the evil one, but it will take a lifetime and longer to learn all the Spirit has to teach. And this brings us to your death, or my death if you prefer.

After laying there in the grave getting some much needed sound sleep, there will come a day when Jesus returns to earth to claim those who loved and obeyed Him. All of us saints napping will arise to meet Him in the air along with those who are the living righteous at the time. Here is the sad part. While Jesus is there, the rest of the dead arises together with the living disobedient, and they will be judged. However, those with our Savior will be whisked away to our reward in Heaven to live forever in perfect peace, joy, and happiness, with absolute love and contentment. We will bask in the warm presence of God the Father and God the Son and God the Holy Spirit. But I am getting ahead of myself.

Chapter 23

Endings

El necio está lleno de muchas palabras
— Biblia, Eclesiastés 10:14a

The foolish are full of words
— Bible, Ecclesiastes 10:14a. (Bible in Basic
English, BBE)

I CAN'T BELIEVE HOW LONG THIS LETTER HAS BECOME! IT set me aback when you announced you were moving out. I remember feeling numb and unprepared and frankly a bit panicked. An obsessive thought kept running through my mind, "have I finished teaching her everything I know?" This question haunted me for several weeks, and finally, in a huff, I decided to write you this letter and go over all I have learned about how to live this ruff-n-tumble life. You know how I love to talk, and I have discovered I love to write too.

I am amazed at how much we, as humans, seem to know intuitively. I have been all over this country to both high-brow and low-brow places, and I have never met anyone who did not know there is a God who created everything and that his crowning creation was Man and Woman. Everyone knows Man and Woman are inherently different from and superior to all other living things. The history of humanity testifies we have always sought to explore and understand the world in which we find ourselves. Further, it has been self-evident from the beginning, humankind was given free will and is self-determined. Without any apparent outside instruction, humanity has known both good and evil, and not only knows both but also knows that *good* is better! And finally, it is common knowledge the world over that the Bible is an essential book despite its perceived mysteriousness.

I am amazed at how little study of the Bible it took to discover the meaning and purpose of life. I found life is all about love, loving God, ourselves, and those we encounter in our life. The Bible offers instructions on how to tend to these relationships and the role the Church (remember, the Church is the assembly of believers) plays in our Father's plan to meet these needs. Another significant discovery was how Jesus provides a way for us to connect to our heavenly Father forever. I found it extremely interesting the way, so many parts of this physical world seem to operate rhythmically, and the Bible seems to be aware of these systems offering instruction on how to live in accord with these systems. Who knew that all those rules about treating other people well do us more good than the other people? Finally, the Bible provides a beautiful picture of words describing the spirit world and our life, our reward, after this one.

So, my love, I fervently hope I have accomplished what I set out to do. With these many words, may you find your key to peace and joy, health and happiness, and always love amidst the ignorance and evil, which so often pollutes this world. In the end, may you find your way home. But I am getting **behind** myself.

It is with joyful pain and hopes for the future that I end this letter.

Love Always, Dad.

Es con dolor mezclado con alegría y esperanza por el futuro que termino esta carta.
Amor para Siempre, Papá.

P.S. Always keep this at the back of your mind for humility's sake. I know I try.

> "One's belief that one is sincere is not so dangerous as one's conviction that one is right. We all feel we are right, but we felt the same way twenty years ago, and today we know we weren't always right."—Igor Stravinsky, Conversations with Igor Stravinsky (1959).[1]

Disclaimer. A human has written this letter. Only the portions, which are direct quotations from the Bible, are valid sources of information and instruction. Everything else is a feeble attempt to grasp God's Holy will.

APPENDICES

#1

Hierarchy of your relationships and responsibilities

God

Self

Spouse

Children

Church family

Parents and In-laws

Siblings

Nieces and Nephews

Grandparents

Aunts and Uncles

Cousins

Non-Christian friends

Acquaintances

Strangers

E.T.

(A reaction to the Bible, Matthew 22:36-40.)

#2

Some Biblical Names and Titles of God

God

Star

I Am

Rock

Lord

YHWH

Light

Stone

Power

Elohim

My Cup

Yahweh

Father

Shield

Potter

Refuge

Heaven

Creator

Jehovah

Husband

Fortress

The King

Shepherd

Redeemer

Holy One

Sovereign

Holy Spirit

Cornerstone

Upright One

The Majesty

Hiding Place
Abba (Daddy)
I Am That I Am
Prince of Peace
Ancient of Days
A Consuming Fire
Tower of Strength
The Divine Nature
Wonderful Counselor
The Law Giver and Judge
The Eternal Immortal Invisible King
Father of our Lord Yeshua the Messiah

#3

Some Biblical Names and Titles of Jesus

God	I Am
Master	Messiah
Servant	The Son
The Life	The Word
The Door	Holy One
Firstborn	Son of God
Son of Man	Lamb of God
The Mediator	The Last Adam
Lion of Judah	The True Vine
Chief Shepherd	The Bridegroom
Prince of Life	The Word of God
The Word of Life	King of the Jews
Chief Cornerstone	Only Begotten Son
Savior of All Men	Son of the Father
The Bread of Life	Yeshua of Nazareth
Light of the World	The Great High Priest
Immanuel (God with us)	Firstborn from the Dead
The Bright Morning Star	Firstborn of all Creation
The Beginning and the End	The Image of the Invisible God
King of Kings and Lord of Lords	The Way, The Truth, and The Life
The Head of the Body, The Church	Advocate, Counsel for the Defender

#4

Some Biblical Names and Titles of satan

rulers of the darkness of this world

prince of the power of the air

the accuser of the brethren

prince that shall come

prince of this world

the great deceiver

father of all lies

power of darkness

god of this world

that old serpent

son of perdition

king of Babylon

prince of Tyrus

the wicked one

angel of light

the adversary

king of Tyrus

the proud one

the evil one

the tempter

little horn

man of sin

the enemy

beelzebub

the devil

apollyon

abaddon

THE TRUTH WE ALREADY KNEW

lucifer

serpent

dragon

belial

satan

REFERENCES

Chapter One:

1) Ben W. Hunt, *Indian Crafts, and Lore* (Milwaukee, WI: Bruce Publishing Co., 1954).

2) Rudolf Flesch, *The Art of Clear Thinking* (New York: NY: Harper and Brothers Publishers, 1951).

3) Janette Sebring Lowrey, The Pokey Little Puppy (Racine, WI: Simon and Schuster; Western Printing and Lithographing Co., 1942).

4) Carl Sagan, *Cosmos* (New York: Random House, 1980).

5) Sir Fredrick Hoyle BBC Radio: 1830 GMT on 28 March 1949.

6) Sir Fredrick Hoyle and Chandra Wickramasinghe, *Evolution from Space: A Theory of Cosmic Creationism* (New York, NY: Touchstone Books, Simon & Schuster, 1981).

7) Stephen J. Gould, Ph.D., The Structure of Evolutionary Theory (Cambridge, MA: Harvard University Press, 2002).

8) Stanley L. Miller, Ph.D., http://www.accessexcellence. org/WN/NM/miller.php

9) John D. Barrow, *The Anthropic Cosmological Principle* (New York, NY: Oxford University Press Inc., 1988).

Chapter Two:

1) Jeffrey Kluger, Jeff Chu/ London, Broward Liston/ Orlando, Maggie Sieger/ Chicago, and Daniel Williams/ Sydney, "Religion: Is God in our Genes?" *Time* (Monday, October 25, 2004).

2) Israel Finkelstein and Neil Asher Silberman, "The Bible Unearthed: Archaeology's New Vision of Ancient Israel and the Origin of its Sacred Texts," http://nytimes.com/ books/first/f/finkelst ein-bible.html

3) Michael D. Lemonick, *"Are the Bible's Stories True?"* Time (December 18, 1995.)

4) http://www.worldnetdaily.com/muchabouthistory/ph araohschariotsfoundinredsea/joekovacs/june212003
5) http://www.carm.org/manuscript-evidence/mattslick
6) http://destinationyisrael.biblesearchers.com/ destination-yisrael/2010/07/the-jewish-torah-roots-of-the-american-constitution-by-prof-paul-eidelberg.html

Chapter Three:
1) Larry Stone, *"The Story of the Bible: The Fascinating History of Its Writing, Translation, and Effect on Civilization" (Nashville, TN: Thomas Nelson, 2010).*
2) http://www.staticbrain.com/bibles-printed
3) http://www.bible-researcher.com/greatest-english-classic/cleland-boyd-mcafee-D.D.
4) Bernard Ramm, *"Protestant Christian Evidences"* (Chicago, IL: Moody, 1953).
5) Lee Strobel, "The Case For Christ" (Grand Rapids, MI: Zondervan Publishing House, 1998).
6) Otto Kaiser, "The Old Testament Apocrypha: An Introduction" (Peabody, MA: Hendrickson Publishers, 2004).
7) J.K. Elliott, "The Apocryphal New Testament" (New York, NY: Oxford University Press Inc., 1993).
8) Phillip Schaff and David Schley Schaff, "History of the Christian Church" (New York, NY: Charles Scribner's Sons, 1910).
9) Michael J. Kruger, "Cannon Revisited: Establishing the Origins and Authority of the New Testament Books" (Wheaton, IL: Crossway, 2012).
10) Robert M. Schoch, *"Voyages of the Pyramid Builders"* (New York, NY: Jeremy P. Tarcher/Penguin (a member of Penguin Group (USA) Inc. New York, 2003).

11) Robert Spencer, "The Truth About Muhammad: Founder of the World's Most Intolerant Religion" (Washington, DC: Regnery Press, 2006).

Chapter Four:
1) William Whiston, *"The Complete Works of Josephus"* (Grand Rapids, MI: Kregel Publications,1999).
2) Carius Cornelius Tacitus, *"The Histories of Tacitus"* (Charleston, SC: BiblioBazaar Books, 2010).
3) Gaius Suetonius Tranquillus, *"The Twelve Caesars"* (Auckland, New Zealand: The Floating Press, 2009).
4) Lucian of Samosata, translated by H.W. and F.G. Fowler *"The Death of Peregrine"* (New York, NY: Digireads Publishing, 2012)

Chapter Five:
1) http://www.nrb.org/news_room/articles/ravi-zacharias-speaks-at-un-prayer-breakfast/

Chapter Six:
1) http://www.hirr.hartsem.edu/research/fastfacts/fast_facts.html
2) Steven L. Nock, Laura Ann Sanchez, James D. Wright, *"Covenant Marriage: The Movement to Reclaim Tradition in America"* (Piscataway, NJ: Rutgers University Press, 2008).

Chapter Seven:
1) Thomas Anthony Harris, I'm OK-You're OK," New York, NY: Harper & Row Press, 1967).

Chapter Eight:

1) Ravi Zacharias, *"Jesus Among Other Gods: The Absolute Claims of the Christian Message"* (Nashville, TN: W Publishing Group, 2000).

2) Henry Kissinger, *"Diplomacy"* (New York, NY: Simon & Schuster, 1994).

Chapter Nine:

3) Anne Casselman, *"The largest living organism in the world, is a fungus,"* Scientific American (October 2007).

Chapter Ten:

Chapter Eleven:

1) The Addams Family. ABC. Filmways, Inc. Hollywood. 1964. Television. Theme song. Written, arranged, and performed by Vic Mizzy.

2) Timbuk3. *The Future's so Bright.* I.R.S., 1986. Nashville, TN. CD.

3) Evita and "Don't Cry for me Argentina," written by Andrew Lloyd Webber and lyricist Tim Rice. Dir. Harold Prince. Starring and sung by Patti LuPone. September 25, 1979. Act II, 25. & Evita. Dir. Alan Parker. Perf. Madonna, Antonio Banderas. December 25, 1996. Hollywood Pictures and Cenergi Pictures. Film.

Chapter Twelve:

Chapter Thirteen

1) http://www.prb.org/Publications/Articles/2002/ HowManyPeopleHaveEverLivedon Earthaspx

2) *Robin Hood: Prince of Thieves.* Dir. Kevin Reynolds. Perf. Kevin Costner, Morgan Freeman, Mary Elizabeth

Mastrantonio. Warner Brothers, Morgan Creek Productions, 1991. Film.

Chapter Fourteen:
1) http://www.pewsocialtrends.org/2010/11/18/the-decline–of-marriage-and-rise-of-new-families/2/#ii-overview
2) http://www.divorcepad.com/rate/
3) http:www.pewsocialtrends.org/

Chapter Fifteen:
1) Alighieri Dante, tr. to English by Reverend H.F. Cary, 1814 *"Divine Comedy"* Inscription over the entrance to hell. (Boston, MA: MobileReference.com, 2010).

Chapter Sixteen:
1) Ninth Public Hearing, April 8, 2004. Hart Senate Office Building. Washington, DC. Chaired by Thomas Kean. Room 216. 9:03a.m.
2) Voltaire, tr. Roger Pearson, *"Candide and other stories, (Zadig)"* (New York, NY: Oxford University Press Inc., 2006).

Chapter Seventeen:

Chapter Eighteen:
1) http://www.school_survival.net/articles/school/history/compulsory_government_ education php

Chapter Nineteen:
1) Vincent Phillip Muñoz, *"God and the Founders: Madison, Washington, and Jefferson"* (New York: Cambridge University Press, 2009).

2) Tony Williams, *Hurricane of Independence, the untold story of the deadly storm at the deciding moment of the American Revolution"* (Naperville, IL: Sourcebooks, Inc., 2008).

3) Charles Francis Adams, editor *The Works of John Adams, Second President of the United States*, Vol. VIII, To the Officers of the First Brigade of the Third Division of the Militia of Massachusetts. 11 October 1798.) (Boston, MA: Little, Brown, 1854.),

4) Christopher Ezeh, *"The Disaster of the Absence of Moral and Religious Education in the American Public Schools"* (Bloomington, IN Xlibris Corporation, 2010).

5) Oliver Wendell Holmes, Jr. *(1897, January)*. Boston University School of Law. Boston Massachusetts. *"Boston Law School Magazine, 1896-1897, Volume 1, Number, 4 February 1897."* Speech.

Chapter Twenty:

1) International Committee of the Red Cross, edited by Jean Pictet, *"The Geneva Conventions of 12 August 1949, Geneva Convention relative to the Treatment of Prisoners of War. Volume 3 of the Geneva Conventions of 12 August 1949"* (Geneva, Switzerland: International Committee of the Red Cross, 1960).

2) Stanley Meisler, *"United Nations: A History"* (NY, NY: Grove Press, 2011).

3) Stanley Meisler, *"United Nations: A History"* (NY, NY: Grove Press, 2011).

4) http://www.un.org/en/documents/charter

5) Edited by Gudmundur Alfredsson and Asbjorn Eide, *"Universal Declaration of Human Rights: A Common Standard of Achievement" (Leiden, Netherlands: Martinus Nijhoff Publishers, 1999).*

6) JimmyCarterlibrary.gov/documents/inaugural_address. pdf.

7) Stanley Meisler, *"United Nations: A History"* (NY, NY: Grove Press, 2011).

8) Voltaire, tr Roger Pearson, *"Voltaire Almighty: A Life in Pursuit of Freedom"* (New York, NY: Bloomberg Publishing, 2010).

9) United States Bureau of Justice Services (http://www. BJS.gov) and United States Census Bureau (http://www. USCensusBureau.gov).

10) http://www.state.gov/j/drl/rls/hrrpt/humanrightsreport/ index.htm#wrapper

11) William J. Lederer and Eugene Burdick, *"The Ugly American"* (New York, NY: W.W. Norton & Company Inc., 1958).

12) (unknown). Edited by Dena Goodman, *"Marie Antoinette: Writings on the Body of a Queen"* (NY, NY: Routledge, 2003).

13) Malcolm Brown and Shirley Seaton, *"Christmas Truce: The Western Front 1914"* (London N1 9RR: Pan Macmillan, 2011).

Chapter Twenty-One:

1) http://www.unmuseum.org/nazca.htm

2) Preston Dennett, Edited by Rosemary Ellen Guiley, *"UFOs and Aliens. Mysteries, Legends, and Unexplained Phenomena"* (N.Y., NY: Chelsea House Publishing, 2008).

3) http://www.defense.gov/transcripts/transcript. aspx?transcriptid=458

4) http://www.ufoevidence.org/topics/unitednations.htm

5) http://www.ufoevidence.org/topics/unitednations.htm

Chapter Twenty-Two:

1) Dylan Thomas, *"Dylan Thomas: Selected Poems"* (NY, NY: New Directions, 1953).

Chapter Twenty-Three:

1) Igor Stravinsky and Robert Craft, *"Conversations with Igor Stravinsky"* (Garden City, NY: Doubleday Company, Inc., 1959).